C39Rom

NEW
Signed

S0-BBH-118

C39Rom

Robert Webster

Mike Webster

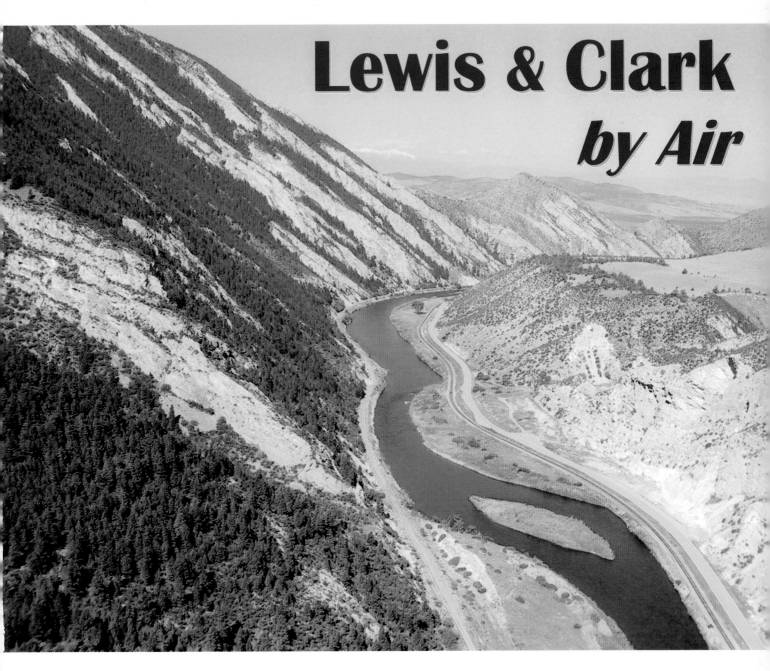

Lewis & Clark by Air

A Pictorial Tour of the Historic Lewis and Clark Trail

by Bob and Mike Webster

Copyright © 2003 by ViaPlanes, Ltd.
600 SE 49th
Pryor, OK 74361

ISBN 0-9728942-0-9
Printed in Korea

www.LewisAndClarkByAir.com

Lewis and Clark by Air

Introduction

On April 14, 1804, the Lewis and Clark Expedition began their journey from the mouth of the Missouri River to the Pacific Ocean with 40 to 46 men and three boats. People cheered from the banks as Lewis and Clark left St. Charles, near St. Louis. The group returned more than two years later, after a long, arduous, and successful exploration.

The expedition had two captains of equal rank, Meriwether Lewis and William Clark. There were three sergeants, Floyd, Ordway, and Pryor. (Gass later replaced Floyd, who died near Sioux City, Iowa, probably from appendicitis.) A few years after their return, Sergeant Nathaniel Pryor established a trading post in northeastern Oklahoma. He married an Osage woman, had children, and lived the rest of his life in the settlement that later became today's town of Pryor, Oklahoma.

Approximately 198 years and 53 days after the launch of the Lewis and Clark expedition, two of us, Bob and Mike Webster, departed our homes in Pryor for St. Louis and then on to the Pacific Ocean, following the trail of Lewis and Clark. Our expedition had two people and one airplane. Instead of more than two years, we took just three weeks to get to the Pacific and back. Hardly anybody noticed, let alone cheered, as we took off to the north.

The main purpose of our expedition was to have fun, but as long as we were going we decided we would take some pictures for a book. With recent advances in modern digital cameras, we were able to take thousands of quality photographs. Well, we took at least a *few* quality photographs. We included the good ones in this book, along with some interesting but mediocre photos. We thought it would be keeping with William Clark's tradition of horrible spelling to offer aerial photos that include the occasional airplane tire.

The Plane

We flew an unusual plane on our trip. The Aircam was originally designed by Phil Lockwood for filming wildlife in Africa for National Geographic. A homebuilt aircraft, the Aircam is sold as a kit. Ours took three people six months to construct. More information on the plane can be found on page 266.

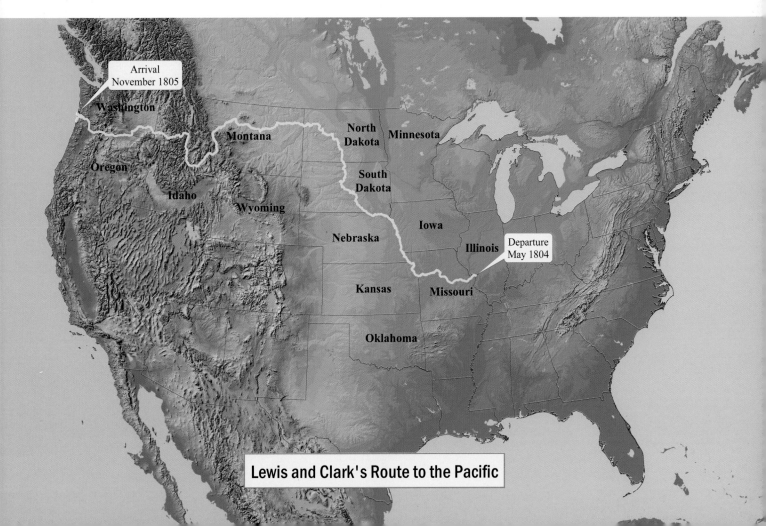

Lewis and Clark's Route to the Pacific

The Photography

All photographs in this book were taken in the air from the Aircam, with the exception of those photos taken *of* the plane. We followed the route of Lewis and Clark, so most of the pictures in the book were taken viewing toward the Pacific Ocean — upstream on the Missouri and downstream on the Columbia. The captions on the "backward" pictures mention their direction of view. All the pictures in the book, except a few of the Aircam, were taken from June 7 through June 15, 2002. The photographs in this book are in their "natural" form without color enhancement.

With each photo there is a date and a mile number. The date is the day the expedition passed the place in the photo. Lewis and Clark sometimes traveled ahead of the main group, so occasionally the dates of their journal excerpts do not match the dates with the photos.

The mile numbers with the photos are the number of miles from the expedition's starting point at the mouth of the Missouri River. Clark's mileage measurements were a little high sometimes, but we used his numbers anyway because he was first. For reference, we used Martin Plamondon II's *Lewis and Clark Trail Maps*.

Journal Excerpts

Throughout the book we've included excerpts from the journals of Captains Lewis and Clark, and Sergeants Ordway, Gass, and Floyd, and Private Whitehouse. Sergeant Pryor also wrote a journal, but it was apparently lost before it was published. We corrected most of their creative spelling and grammatical errors. Clark was particularly liberal in his spelling, capitalization, and punctuation. We did not correct some of the minor factual mistakes in the journal entries. For example, Clark once mentioned that he heard a nightingale sing all night. It was probably a mockingbird, brown thrasher, or catbird, because no species of nightingale is found in North America.

If you want to read the original journals, an excellent source is *The Definitive Journals of Lewis and Clark*, edited by Gary Moulton and published in 2002. It includes the complete journals with many corrections, references, and informative footnotes. A cheaper, somewhat less informative set of the journals was published by Reuben Thwaites in 1904, titled *Original Journals of the Lewis and Clark Expedition*. A good condensed version of the journals by Bernard DeVoto is available, *The Journals of Lewis and Clark*. You can also find the unedited journals of Lewis and Clark on the internet at www.LewisAndClarkByAir.com.

The Journey

The aerial perspective of this book offers a unique viewpoint of the Lewis and Clark Trail. Traveling by plane gives access to many otherwise inaccessible places, and enables a broad view of many confined locations. One of the most interesting aspects of our journey was the contrast in the country 200 years ago and today, in some cases a great difference and in others almost none.

Acknowledgements

Many thanks to our underworked, overpaid, alleged editor Leann Burger, without whom there would be even more errors in this book than there are, and to everyone else who helped us in this effort.

Getting Started...

Across Missouri

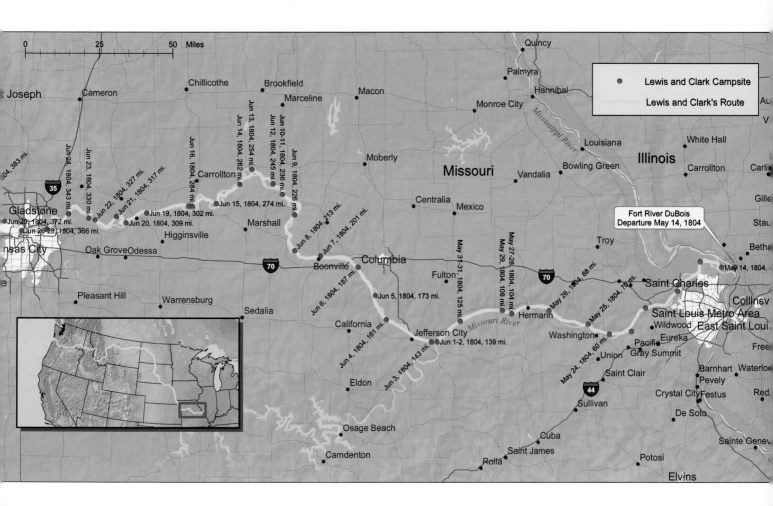

On May 14, 1804 the Lewis and Clark Expedition left camp near St. Louis to begin their journey to the Pacific Ocean.

After taking off from Greensfield, Missouri, we flew to the mouth of the Missouri River and followed the route of Lewis and Clark to the Pacific Ocean. It took us eight days, usually flying from 60 to 80 mph. We spent two of the eight days on the ground because of wind, rain, and low clouds. It took the Lewis and Clark Expedition 862 days to travel that distance and return, including the two winters they laid over.

May 13, 1804, mile 0

On May 14, 1804, the Lewis and Clark Expedition set out from Camp River Dubois where they had stayed since the previous December. Camp River Dubois was on the east side of the Mississippi River when Lewis and Clark camped there. Since then, the river channel has shifted and that location is now on the west side of the river in a flood plain, in the foreground of this picture.

May 13, 1804, mile 0

All our provisions, goods, and equipage are on board a boat of 22 oars, a large pirogue of 7 oars, and a second pirogue of 6 oars, complete with sails, etc. The men are complete with powder cartridges and 100 balls each, all in health and readiness to set out. The boats and everything are complete, with the necessary stores of provisions and such articles of merchandise as we thought ourselves authorized to procure, though not as much as I think necessary for the multitude of Indians through which we must pass on our road across the continent.

Clark, May 13, 1804

May 13, 1804, mile 0

Industrial plants such as this oil refinery line the east side of the Mississippi near the site of Camp River Dubois.

We set out from Camp River a Dubois at 4 o'clock and proceeded up the Missouri under sail to the first island in the Missouri, and camped on the upper point opposite a creek on the south side, below a ledge of limestone rock called colewater. We made 4½ miles.

Clark, May 14, 1804

In this view to the south, the Missouri River, on the right, flows into the Mississippi. Lewis and Clark camped directly across from the mouth of the Missouri River over winter of 1803-1804. Today, the Missouri flows into the Mississippi 2 miles downstream from their campsite.

May 13, 1804, mile 0

The expedition stopped at the village of St. Charles and camped near the site of the Interstate 70 Bridge and this riverboat casino. They spent four days here, waiting for Lewis to join them from St. Louis and conducting some last minute business. One night during their stay, Werner, Hall, and Collins left the camp without permission and went to a ball. The three of them were court martialed, and Collins, who behaved "in an unbecoming manner," received "50 lashes on his naked back."

May 21, 1804, mile 24

May 22, 1804, mile 38

We arrived at St. Charles and passed the evening with a great deal of satisfaction, all cheerful and in good spirits. This place is an old French village situated on the north side of the Missouri. The people are dressy, polite people and Roman Catholics.
Whitehouse May 16, 1804

This bridge under construction is part of the Page Avenue Extension project near Creve Coeur Lake.

The Daniel Boone Bridge (above) crosses the Missouri near Weldon, Missouri. The expedition visited a camp of Kickapoo Indians just upstream from this bridge.

May 22, 1804, mile 27

May 15, 1804, mile 5

Today, several bridges span the Missouri in the St. Louis area. Lewis and Clark had to travel thousands of miles before they could walk across the river.

The Lewis Bridge on Highway 67.

We set out at half past 3 o'clock under three cheers from the gentlemen on the bank.

Clark, May 21, 1804

We passed several small farms on the bank, and a large creek on the larboard side called Bon Homme. A camp of Kickapoos was on the starboard side. Those Indians told me several days ago that they would come on and hunt, and by the time I got to their camp they would have some provisions for us. Soon after we came to, the Indians arrived with four deer as a present, for which we gave them two quarts of whiskey.

Clark, May 22, 1804

May 23, 1804, mile 48

On May 18, 1804, four days after the expedition departed, Napoleon crowned himself Emperor of France.

May 23, 1804, mile 48

We proceeded to the mouth of a creek on the starboard side called Osage Woman's River, opposite a large island and settlement. We took in R and Jo Fields, who had been sent to purchase corn, butter, etc. Many people came to see us.

We passed a large cave on the larboard side, called by the French *Tavern*, about 120 feet wide, 40 feet deep, and 20 feet high. Many different images are painted on the rock at this place. The Indians and French pay homage. Many names are written on the rock.

Captain Lewis was near falling from the pinnacles of rocks 300 feet high. He caught at 20 feet, saved himself by the assistance of his knife.

Clark, May 23, 1804

Tavern Cave is in this area, across the river from Defiance, Missouri. Lewis was probably on one of these rocks when he almost fell 300 feet.

The expedition bought butter and corn at Boone's Settlement, the home of Daniel Boone and 30 to 40 families. Boone's Settlement was located near today's town of Defiance.

We passed a very bad part of the river called the Devil's Race Ground. This is where the current sets against some projecting rocks for half a mile on the larboard side. Above this place is the mouth of a small creek called Quivre. We attempted to pass up under the larboard bank which was falling in so fast that the evident danger obliged us to cross between the starboard side and a sand bar in the middle of the river.

We hove up near the head of the sand bar, the same moving and backing caused us to run on the sand. The swiftness of the current wheeled the boat. It broke our tow rope, and was nearly oversetting the boat. All hands jumped out on the upper side and bore on that side until the sand washed from under the boat, and wheeled on the next bank.

By the time she wheeled a 3rd time we got a rope fast to her stern and by the means of swimmers was carried to shore. When her stern was down whilst in the act of swinging a third time into deep water near the shore, we returned to the Island where we set out and ascended under the bank which I have just mentioned as falling in. We camped about 1 mile above where we were so nearly being lost, on the larboard side at a plantation, all in spirits. This place I call the retrograde bend as we were obliged to fall back 2 miles.

Clark, May 24, 1804

May 24, 1804, mile 54

Today's river has shifted about a mile to the north of Devil's Race Ground. The Labadie Power Plant now lies in the 1804 river channel. Quivre Creek is now called Labadie Creek and is used for cooling in the power plant.

May 24, 1804, mile 52

We sometimes think of bank erosion as a modern problem, but it is a natural occurrence that Lewis and Clark encountered throughout their voyage.

May 25, 1804, mile 67

This dredge helps keep the river clear of sandbars and shallows. Washington, Missouri is in the background.

May 25, 1804, mile 66

The Highway 47 Bridge links Washington, Missouri to the north side of the river.

May 25, 1804, mile 67

Near the modern-day town of Washington, Lewis and Clark stopped at a French village of seven families called St. Johns. Sergeant Floyd wrote that this was "the last white settlement on the river."

May 25, 1804, mile 67

We camped at the mouth of a creek called River la Charrette, above a French village of 7 houses and as many families. They settled at this place to be convenient to hunt and trade with the Indians. The people in this village are poor and the houses are small. They sent us milk and eggs to eat.

Clark, May 25, 1804

The Missouri meanders through the wide river bottom. Streaks through the fields show where the river has changed its course over the years. Today's river is narrower, straighter, and deeper in most places, having been modified for navigation. Even 200 years ago people were using this part of the river for transportation.

As we were pushing off this morning two canoes loaded with fur came to from the Omaha nation, which place they had left two months ago. [The Omaha nation was 730 miles up the river.] At about 10 o'clock 4 cajeux or rafts loaded with furs and pelts came to, one from the Pawnees and the others from the Grand Osage. They informed nothing of consequence.
Clark, May 27, 1804

In the space of one hundred and seventy-six years the Lower Mississippi has shortened itself two hundred and forty-two miles. This is an average of a trifle over 1 miles and a third per year. Therefore, any calm person, who is not blind or idiotic, can see that in the Old Oolithic Silurian Period, just a million years ago next November, the Lower Mississippi River was upwards of one million three hundred thousand miles long, and stuck out over the Gulf of Mexico like a fishing rod. And by the same token any person can see that seven hundred and forty-two years from now the Lower Mississippi will be only a mile and three quarters long, and Cairo and New Orleans will have joined there streets together, and be plodding comfortably along under a single mayor and a mutual board of aldermen.
Mark Twain, 1883
Life on the Mississippi

May 26, 1804, mile 77

The Union Pacific Railroad
follows the south side of the
Missouri almost the entire
distance from St. Louis to
Kansas City.

May 26, 1804, mile 77

May 27, 1804, mile 89

The popular Katy Bike Trail
follows the north side of the
Missouri for about 150 miles.
With a total length of 225
miles, it is the longest rails-to-
trails conversion in the U.S.

This view of the Missouri shows the railroad on the left, a small boat in the center, and the Hermann airport at the upper right.

May 27, 1804, mile 97

May 27, 1804, mile 98

Hermann, Missouri was founded in 1837 by German settlers, 35 years after Lewis and Clark passed by. A small town with fewer than 3,000 residents, Hermann's Highway 19 Bridge, city boat ramp, railroad, and airport show transportation advances unheard of in 1804. A year before the expedition, Lewis traveled on the most modern highway in the United States, from Lancaster to Philadelphia, Pennsylvania. Stages averaged an amazing 5 to 7 mph on the country's first gravel road.

May 27, 1804, mile 101

As I was hunting this day I came across a cave on the south side or fork of a river about 100 yards from the river. I went 100 yards under ground had with no light in my hand. If I had, I should have gone further. There was a small spring in it. It is the most remarkable cave I ever saw in my travels.

Whitehouse, May 27, 1804

June 4, 1804, mile 151

Several deer were killed today. At the mouth of Moreau Creek I saw much sign of war parties of Indians having crossed from the mouth of this creek. I have a bad cold and a sore throat.

Clark, June 3, 1804

Barges on the Missouri River typically transport grain, rock, fertilizer, and other bulk products.

June 1, 1804, mile 135

May 30, 1804, mile 111

The Missouri State Capitol overlooks the Missouri River in Jefferson City.

We passed a small creek at 1 mile, 15 yards wide, and named it Nightingale Creek from a bird of that description which sang for us all last night, and is the first of the kind I ever heard.
Clark, June 4, 1804

June 4, 1804, mile 147

June 5, 1804, mile 171

A train travels down the river near Mine Hill, south of Marion, Missouri. The hunters of the expedition killed seven deer the day they passed here. That seems like a lot, but they were feeding more than 40 people at the time.

Wide above some small islands we passed a creek on the larboard side about 15 yards wide, Mast Creek. Here the Sergeant at the helm ran under a bending tree and broke the mast. This is some delightful land, with a gentle ascent about this creek, well timbered in Oak, Ash, Walnut, etc.
Clark, June 4, 1804

I got out and walked on the larboard side through a rush bottom for 1 mile and a short distance through. Nettles were as high as my breast. I ascended a hill of about 170 feet to a place where the French report that lead ore has been found. I saw no mineral of that description.

Captain Lewis camped immediately under this hill, to wait, which gave me some time to examine the hill. On the top is a mound about six feet high, and about 100 acres of land on which the large timber is dead. In descending about 50 feet there is a projecting limestone rock under which is a cave. At one place in these projecting rocks I went on one which spurred up and hung over the water. From the top of this rock I had a prospect of the river for 20 or 30 miles up.

Our hunters killed 7 deer today.

Clark, June 4, 1804

June 7, 1804, mile 190

We mended our mast this morning and set out at 7 o'clock under a gentle breeze from the southeast by south. We passed a large island and a creek called Split Rock Creek. At 5 miles on the starboard side we passed the rock from which this Creek, 20 yards wide, takes its name: a projecting rock with a hole through.

The banks are falling in very much today. The river rose last night a foot. We saw some buffalo signs today.

Clark, June 6, 1804

June 7, 1804, mile 189

The Katy Bike Trail passes beneath the limestone bluffs near Rocheport, Missouri. Split Rock Creek is now called Perchee Creek, and enters the Missouri about three miles below its mouth of 1804.

Interstate 70 crosses the Missouri near Moniteau Creek, called the "River of the Big Devil" by Sergeant Floyd. Moniteau Creek enters the Missouri at the town of Rocheport, barely visible on the outside of the bend in the distance. Just upstream from Moniteau Creek, the expedition found some Indian paintings on the rocks. These are no longer visible, and may have been blasted away during the construction of the railroad that has since become the Katy Bike Trail.

June 7, 1804, mile 191

We found a dredge boat beneath some power lines, clearing the Missouri River channel.

June 7, 1804, mile 191

We passed some small willow islands and camped at the mouth of a small river called Good Woman's River. This river is about 35 yards wide and is said to be navigable by pirogues for several leagues.

Our hunters brought in three bears this evening, and informed us that the Country through which they passed from the last creek is fine, rich land, and well watered.

Clark, June 7, 1804

Highway 40 and a railroad bridge cross the Missouri at Boonville, Missouri upstream from the Bonne Femme River. Clark chose the English translation and called it "Good Woman's River."

June 8, 1804, mile 202

We passed the head of the Island opposite which we camped last night, and ate breakfast at the mouth of a large Creek on the starboard side, 30 yards wide, called Big Moniteau. A Short distance above the mouth of this creek are several curious paintings and carvings on the projecting rock of limestone inlaid with white, red, and blue flint, of a very good quality. The Indians have taken of this flint in great quantities. We landed at this inscription and found it a den of rattlesnakes. We had not landed 3 minutes before three very large snakes were observed in the crevices of the rocks and killed.

Clark, June 7, 1804

June 9, 1804, mile 223

Our shadow on a sandbar.

Today's main river channel is largely free of snags and submerged trees, although sandbars and snags are not unusual outside the main channel. The U.S. Army Corps of Engineers maintains a river channel 300 feet wide and 9 feet deep for commercial barge traffic of rock, grain, fertilizer, and other products. The Missouri is usually closed to barge traffic from early December to late March because of low water. The Mississippi River has 250 times more barge traffic that the Missouri, in terms of ton-miles.

We had like to have stove our boat, in going around a snag her stern struck a log under water and she swung around on the snag with her broad side to the current exposed to the drifting timber. By the active exertions of our party we got her off in a few minutes without injury and crossed to the island where we camped.

Clark, June 9, 1804

June 12, 1804, mile 244

The northwest wind blew hard and cold. As this wind was immediately ahead, we could not proceed. We took advantage of this delay and dried our wet articles, examined provisions, etc. The river began to fall. The hunters killed two deer. Drouillard killed two bears in the prairie. They were not fat. We had the meat jerked, and also the venison. It is a constant practice to have all the fresh meat not used dried in this way.

Clark, June 11, 1804

June 8, 1804, mile 208

A hard rain last night, we set out this morning very early. We passed some bad places in the river, saw a number of goslings this morning, and passed near a bank which was falling in at the time we passed.

Clark, June 10, 1804

Today, geese share the fertile bottomland with farmers in these fields north of Boonville, Missouri.

June 8, 1804, mile 207

This is as handsome
a place as I ever saw in
an uncultivated state.
Glass, June 13, 1804

This photo clearly shows the former river channels. In 1804 the river ran around the bend on the right side of the photo. Here, 200-300 Missouri Indians were killed by the Sauks a few years before Lewis and Clark arrived.

We set out early and passed a round bend to the starboard side and two creeks called the Round Bend Creeks. Between those two creeks and behind a small willow island in the bend is a prairie in which the Missouri Indians once lived, and the spot where 300 of them fell a sacrifice to the fury of the Sauks. This nation, once the most numerous nation in this part of the continent, is now reduced to about 30 families, and that few under the protection of the Otos on the River Platt, who themselves are declining.

Clark, June 13, 1804

A well-used hydrofoil is docked on Grand River near Brunswick, Missouri. The USS Aries was purchased for scrap on an internet auction, but the new owners decided to restore the U.S. Navy missile ship rather than scrap it. Lewis and Clark camped at the mouth of Grand River on June 13. Since then, both rivers have changed course and meet about 2 miles farther to the southwest.

We came to in the mouth of Grand River on starboard side and camped for the night. This river is from 80 to 100 yards wide at its mouth and navigable for pirogues a great distance. This river heads with the River Des Moines. Below its mouth is a beautiful plain of bottomland. The hills rise at a mile back, and the lands about this place are either plain or over flow bottom. Captain Lewis and myself walked to the hill, from the top of which we had a beautiful prospect of the surrounding country. In the open prairie we caught a raccoon. Our hunters brought in a bear and a deer. We took some lunar observations this evening.

Clark, June 13, 1804

June 13, 1804, mile 253

A modern fishing boat speeds up the Missouri 20 times faster than Lewis and Clark.

June 24, 1804, mile 335

June 15, 1804, mile 263

June 15, 1804, mile 273

The Missouri River winds westward across the state.

The country on each side of the river is fine, interspersed with prairies in which immense numbers of deer are seen. On the banks of the river we observe numbers of deer watering and feeding on the young willow, several killed today.

Clark, June 24, 1804

In 1804, Kansas City was uninhabited wilderness.

The Kansas City Downtown Airport lies in the 1804 Missouri riverbed. The modern expressways, airport, and railroads stand in contrast to the hard 9¾ miles the expedition traveled on June 26 to arrive at the current site of downtown Kansas City. Clark saw a great number of Carolina parakeets here. Now they are extinct.

At this place the river appears to be confined in a very narrow channel, and the current still more so by a counter current or whirl on one side and a high bank on the other. We passed a small island in the bend to the larboard side. We killed a large rattlesnake sunning himself on the bank. We passed a bad sand bar where our tow rope broke twice. With great exertions we rowed around it, came to, and camped in the point above the Kansas River. I observed a great number of parroquets this evening. Our party killed seven deer today.

Clark, June 26, 1804

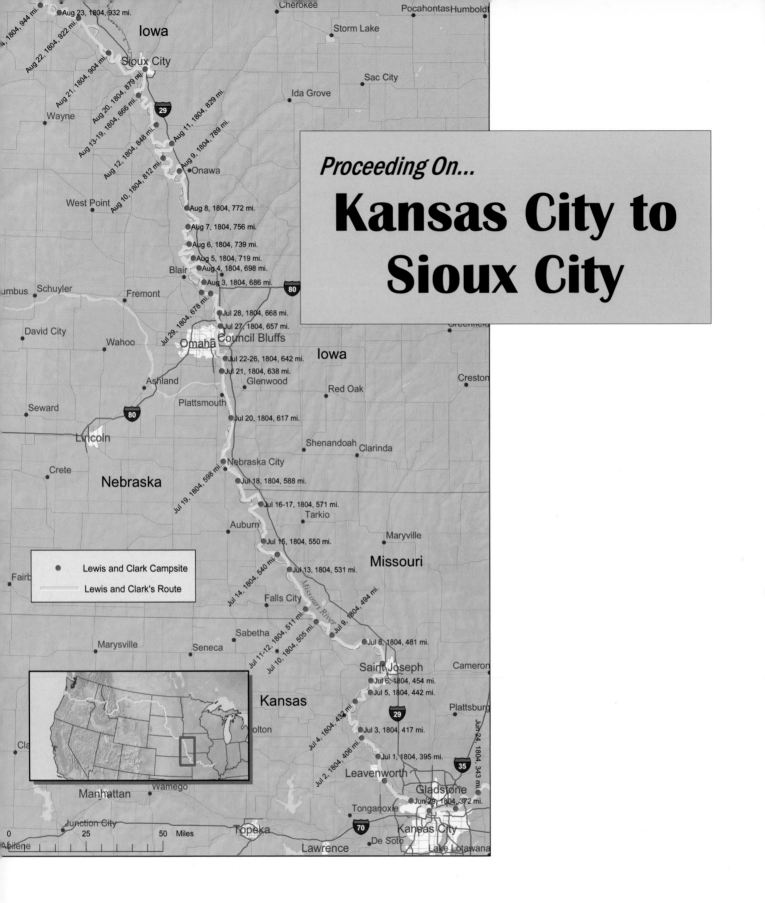

Proceeding On...

Kansas City to Sioux City

From June 29 to August 20 the expedition rowed, sailed, and pulled their boats up the Missouri from the Kansas River to the current location of Sioux City, Iowa.

July 1, 1804, mile 390

Leavenworth Federal Penitentiary is across the river from Tree Frog Island, although the island no longer exists.

Ordered – A Court Martial will set this day at 11 o'clock to consist of five members, for the trial of John Collins and Hugh Hall, confined on charges exhibited against them by Sergeant Floyd, agreeable to the articles of war.

John Potts to act as Judge Advocate.

The Court convened agreeable to order and proceeded to the trial of the Prisoners viz. John Collins charged "with getting drunk on his post this morning out of whiskey put under his charge as a sentinel, and for suffering Hugh Hall to draw whiskey out of the said barrel intended for the party."

To this charge the prisoner pleaded not guilty.

The Court, after mature deliberation on the evidence, adduced and are of the opinion that the prisoner is guilty of the charge exhibited against him, and do therefore sentence him to receive one hundred lashes on his bare back.

Hugh Hall was brought before the Court, charged with "taking whiskey out of a keg this morning which whiskey was stored on the bank (and under the charge of the guard), contrary to all order, rule, or regulation."

To this charge the prisoner pleaded guilty.

The Court find the prisoner Guilty and sentence him to receive fifty lashes on his bare back.

The commanding officers approve of the sentence of the court and orders that the punishment take place at half past three this evening, at which time the party will parade for inspection.

From the Orderly Book, June 29, 1804

We passed on the north side of Diamond Island a small creek mouth opposite I call Biscuit Creek. A large sand bar in the middle of the river 1 ½ miles above the island is covered with driftwood. We came to above this drift and delayed three hours to refresh the men who were very much overpowered with the heat. [It had been 96°F the previous day.] There are great quantities of grapes and raspberries. We passed a small creek on the larboard side below one large and two small islands. This creek and island are called Remore (or Tree Frog). A large pond is on the starboard side, the main current of water running on the larboard side of the island. I am told that three years ago the main current ran on the starboard side of the island and there was no appearance of the two smaller islands. Deer and turkeys are in great quantities on the bank.

Clark, July 1, 1804

After making some arrangements and inflicting a little punishment to two men, we set out at ½ past 4 o'clock and proceeded on.

Clark, June 29, 1804

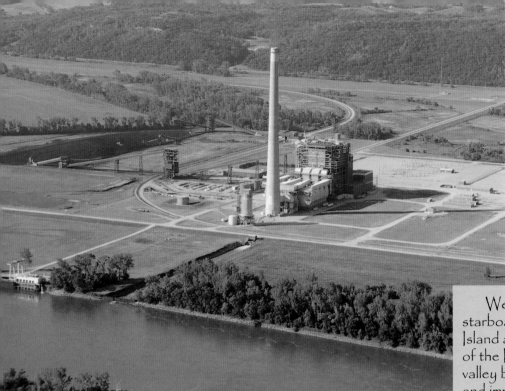

The Iatan Power Plant is just downstream from the July 2 campsite and the abandoned Kansas Indian village, and across the river from the deserted French Garrison that was active around 1757.

July 2, 1804, mile 405

We camped after dark on the starboard side above Bear Medicine Island and opposite the first old village of the Kansas, which was situated in a valley between two points of high land and immediately on the river bank. Back of the village and on a rising ground at about 1 mile the French had a garrison for some time.

Clark, July 2, 1804

We passed two islands, one a small willow island on the larboard side, the other large called by the French Isle de Vache or Cow Island. Opposite the head on the starboard side is a large pond containing beaver and fowl.

Clark, July 3, 1804

July 3, 1804, mile 408

Bean Lake is a remnant of the 1804 river channel at Isle de Vache or Cow Island.

We have in all 46 men July 4th, 4 horses & a Dog.
Clark, July 4, 1804

July 5, 1804, mile 440

July 5, 1804, mile 440

From a distance, the Missouri looks clean and neat. In this close-up you can see how logs and driftwood could be hazardous to navigation.

This is about 3 miles downstream of the expedition's July 5 campsite, southwest of St. Joseph, Missouri.

> I observe a great quantity of summer and fall grapes, berries, and wild roses on the banks. Deer are not so plentiful as usual. There is a great deal of elk signs.
>
> *Clark, July 5, 1804*

Industrial plants line the shore of the Missouri River in southwestern St. Joseph, Missouri.

One man is very sick, struck with the sun. Captain Lewis bled him and gave him niter, which has revived him much.

Clark, July 7, 1804

July 7, 1804, mile 460

Interstate 229, Highway 36, and the Burlington Northern Santa Fe (BNSF) Railroad make a confusing tangle in St. Joseph.

We passed a high handsome prairie on the north side, and killed a wolf and a large wood rat on the bank. The principle difference between it and the common rat is its having hair on its tail.

Gass, July 7, 1804

July 7, 1804, mile 461

July 7, 1804, mile 461

The Union Pacific Bridge in St. Joseph was built in the 1890's. It stays open like this except when in use, which is only about twice a month.

July 8, 1804, mile 477

We came to for dinner at the lower point of a very large island situated near the starboard side. This island is called Nodaway and is the largest I have seen in the river, containing 7,000 or 8,000 acres of land, seldom overflowed. We camped at the head of this island.

Clark, July 8, 1804

Big Nodaway Island is no longer an island, due to river course changes. The "handsome prairie" is now fertile cropland used for wheat, soybeans, and other crops.

July 8, 1804, mile 477

July 9, 1804, mile 483

A fishing boat heads downstream at a speed that would astonish Lewis and Clark.

We set out and passed the head of the island which was situated opposite to our camp last night. A sand bar is at the head. Opposite this island a creek or bayou comes in from a large pond on the starboard side. As our flanking party saw a great number of pike in this pond, I have laid it down with that name annexed.

Clark, July 9, 1804

July 10, 1804, mile 495

We passed a prairie on the south side where several French families had settled and made corn some years ago. They stayed two years. The Indians came frequently to see them and were very friendly.

Floyd, July 9, 1804

Dikes along the Missouri limit the size of the flood plain and help keep the water contained during floods.

July 9, 1804, mile 494

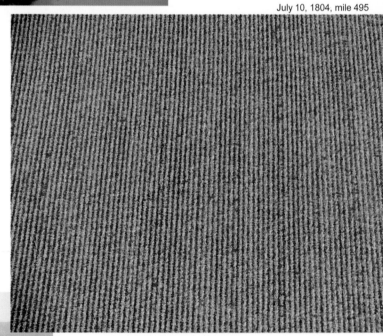

The bottomland along the Missouri makes excellent farmland, but the crop yields are sometimes reduced by floods.

On July 11, 1804, Vice President Aaron Burr shot political adversary Alexander Hamilton in a duel. Hamilton died the following day.

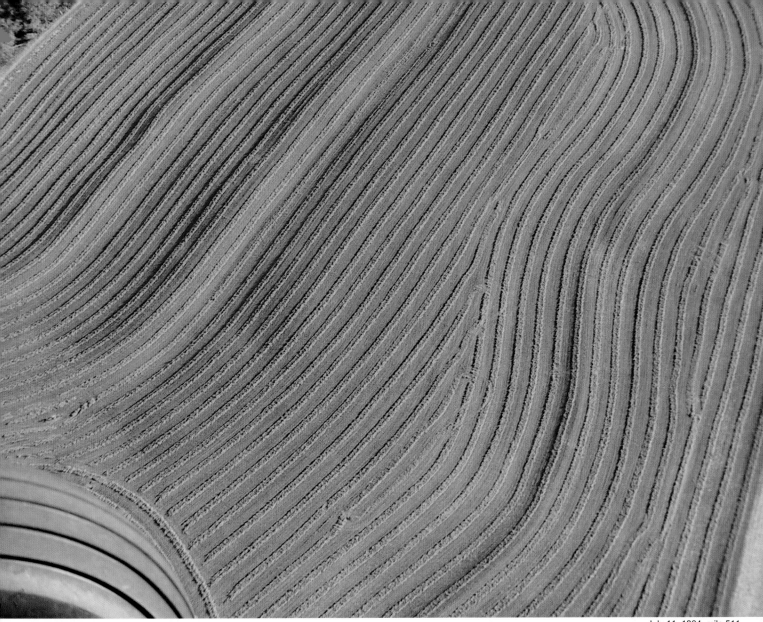

Rows of drying hay appear below our tire.

The atmosphere suddenly darkened by a black and dismal looking cloud. We were in a situation near the upper point of the sand island. On the opposite shore the bank was falling in and lined with snags as far as we could see down. The storm, which passed over an open plain from the northeast, struck our boat on the starboard quarter and would have thrown her up on the sand island, dashed to pieces in an instant, had not the party leaped out on the leeward side and kept her off with the assistance of anchor and cable until the storm was over.

This situation continued about 40 minutes, when the storm suddenly ceased and the river became instantaneously as smooth as glass.

Clark, July 14, 1805

We took a break at the Falls City, Nebraska airport.

July 11, 1804, mile 511

A power line across the Missouri is a mark of civilization as well as a hazard to low-flying aircraft.

July 16, 1804, mile 561

A heavy fog this morning prevented our setting out before 7 o'clock. At nine I took two men and walked on the larboard side. I crossed three beautiful streams of running water heading in the prairies. On those streams the land was very fine, covered with pea vine and rich weed. The high prairies are also good land, covered with grass entirely void of timber, except what grows on the water. I proceeded on through those prairies several miles. In all this day's march through woods and prairies I only saw three deer and three fawns. I saw great quantities of grapes, plums of two kinds, wild cherries of two kinds, hazelnuts, and gooseberries.

Clark, July 15, 1805

We passed a very bad sand bar and encamped on the larboard side at the lower point of the Oven Islands and opposite the prairie, called by the French Four le Tourtere. We saw a dog nearly starved on the bank and gave him some meat. He would not follow. Our hunters killed two deer today.

Clark, July 18, 1804

Faint sulfurous smoke rises from the Nebraska City Station power plant at the expedition's July 18 campsite.

July 18, 1804, mile 588

This is the most open country I ever beheld, almost one continued prairie.

Gass, July 18, 1804

A water skier speeds along Wa Can Da Lake, about 25 miles south of Omaha. This was wolf country in 1804.

July 20, 1804, mile 611

We passed a large willow island on the starboard side and the mouth of a creek about 25 yards wide on the larboard side called by the French *L eau qui Pleure*, or the Water which Cries. This creek falls into the river above a cliff of brown clay opposite the willow island.

I went out above the mouth of this creek and walked the greater part of the day through plains interspersed with small groves of timber on the branches, and some scattering trees about the heads of the runs. I killed a very large yellow wolf. The soil of those prairies appears rich but much parched with the frequent fires.

Clark, July 20, 1804

We arrived at the lower mouth of the great river Platte at 10 o'clock. This great river being much more rapid than the Missouri forces its current against the opposite shore. The current of this river comes with great velocity, rolling its sands into the Missouri, filling up its bed and compelling it to encroach on the starboard shore.

The Platte spreads very wide with many small islands scattered through it, and from its rapidity and rolling sands cannot be navigated with boats or pirogues. The Indians pass this river in skin boats which are flat and will not turn over. The Otos, a small nation, reside on the south side 10 leagues up. The Pawnees are on the same side, 5 leagues higher up.

A great number of wolves are about this evening.

Clark, July 21, 1804

July 21, 1804, mile 637

Offutt Air Force Base, the headquarters of the Strategic Air Command, lies on Lewis and Clark's campsite of July 21.

The Missouri River, Epperly Field, and downtown Omaha, Nebraska. The expedition camped at the north end (on the right) of the airport on July 27, 1804.

July 27, 1804, mile 655

In 1804 the Missouri River passed on the other side of the airport, partially through Carter Lake shown here in the background.

July 27, 1804, mile 655

As we were setting out today one man killed a buck and another cut his knee very bad. We camped in a bend to the larboard side in a copse of trees. There is a very agreeable breeze from the northwest this evening. I killed a deer in the prairie and found the mosquitoes so thick and troublesome that it was disagreeable and painful to continue a moment still.

I took one man, R. Fields, and walked on shore with a view of examining some mounds on the larboard side of the river. Those mounds I found to be of different height, shape, and size, some composed of sand, and some of earth and sand. The highest was next to the river. All covered about 200 acres of land in a circular form. On the side from the river there is a low bottom and small pond. The Otos formerly lived here.

Clark, July 27, 1804

Drouillard brought in a Missouri Indian which he met hunting in the prairie. This Indian is one of the few remaining of that nation, and lives with the Otos. His camp is about 4 miles from the river. He informs that the great gang of the nation were hunting the buffalo in the plains. His party is small, consisting only of about 20 lodges.

Clark, July 28, 1804

The Missouri River in this area is 3 to 5 times narrower than it was in 1804. The Omaha office of the U.S. Army Corps of Engineers has been maintaining Missouri River bank stabilization and navigation since 1882. The Corps of Engineers built rock piers into the river on the inside bank of curves. Silt and material collect between the rocky structures, extending the shoreline into the river and causing a narrower, deeper river. This results in a loss of some of the marshy wetlands and backwaters in exchange for useable land. The rocky piers in this photo were once much longer, not because they protruded farther into the river, but because the river was much wider and extended farther to the left side of the picture. Today the Corps of Engineers is engaged in the Fish and Wildlife Mitigation project, restoring wildlife habitats historically associated with the Missouri River.

In this area, two men disappeared, La Liberté, who was a hired boat hand, and Private Reed, an enlisted man. Reed was considered a deserter.

We sent a French man, La Liberté, with the Indian to the Otos camp to invite the Indians to meet us on the river above.

We stopped to dine under some high trees near the high land on the larboard side. In a few minutes we caught three very large catfish, one nearly white. Those fish are in great plenty on the sides of the river and very fat. A quart of oil came out of the surplus fat of one of those fish.

Above this high land and on the starboard side we passed much falling timber, apparently the ravages of a dreadful hurricane which had passed obliquely across the river from northwest to southeast about twelve months since. Many trees were broken off near the ground, the trunks of which were sound and four feet in diameter. About ¾ of a mile above the island on the starboard side a creek comes in called Boyers River. This creek is 25 yards wide. One man in attempting to cross this creek on a log let his gun fall in. R. Fields dived and brought it up.

Clark, July 29, 1804

Joseph Fields killed and brought in an animal called by the French *blaireau*, and by the Pawnees *cho car tooch*. This animal burrows in the ground and feeds on flesh (prairie dogs), bugs, and vegetables. His shape and size is like that of a beaver. His head, mouth, etc. is like a dog's with short ears. His tail and hair are like that of a ground hog, but longer and lighter. His entrails guts are like the entrails of a hog. His skin is thick and loose. His belly is white and the hair short, with a white streak from his nose to his shoulders. The toenails of his forefeet are one inch and ¾ long, and feet large. The nails of his hind feet are ¾ of an Inch long, the hind feet small and toes crooked. His legs are short and, when he moves, just sufficient to raise his body above the ground. He is of the bear species. We have his skin stuffed.

Several men have very bad boils. Catfish are caught in any part of the river. Turkeys, geese, and a beaver were killed and caught. Every thing is in prime order, the men in high Spirits, and a fair, still evening. There are a great number of mosquitoes this evening.

Clark, July 30, 1804

Captain Lewis and I went up the bank and walked a short distance in the high prairie. This prairie is covered with grass of 10 or 12 inches in height, and the soil is of good quality. At a distance of about a mile still further back the country rises about 80 or 90 feet higher, and is one continued plain as far as can be seen.

From the bluff on the second rise immediately above our camp, the most beautiful prospect of the river up and down and the country opposite presented itself which I ever beheld. The river is meandering the open and beautiful plains, interspersed with groves of timber, and each point is covered with tall timber such as willow, cottonwood, some mulberry, elm, sycamore, linden and ash. The groves contain hickory, walnut, coffee nut and oak in addition. Two ranges of high land lie parallel to each other and from 4 to 10 miles distant, between which the river and its bottoms are contained. The ranges are from 70 to 300 feet high.

Clark, July 30, 1804

The Fort Calhoun Nuclear Power Plant is south of Blair, Nebraska.

August 4, 1804, mile 691

At sunset Mr. Fairfong [a trader resident among the Otos] and a party of the Oto and Missouri Nation came to camp. Among those Indians, six were chiefs (not the principal chiefs). Captain Lewis and myself met those Indians and informed them we were glad to see them, and would speak to them tomorrow. We sent them some rested meat, pork flour, and meal. In return they sent us watermelons. Every man was on his guard, ready for anything.

Clark, August 3, 1804

The two men Drouillard and Colter returned with the horses loaded with elk.

Clark, August 2, 1804

A farmer works across the river from the Fort Calhoun nuclear power plant.

August 4, 1804, mile 691

August 5, 1804, mile 707

This marina outside Blair, Nebraska provides river access for recreational boaters.

August 6, 1804, mile 735

Riverfront homes are common along the Missouri River. This new home is east of Herman, Nebraska.

We stopped for a few minutes in a Nebraska bean field.

August 8, 1804, mile 767

I saw a great number of feathers floating down the river. Those feathers had a very extraordinary appearance, as they appeared in such quantities as to cover pretty generally 60 or 70 yards of the breadth of the river. For 3 miles after I saw those feathers continuing to run in that manner, we did not perceive from whence they came.

At length, we were surprised by the appearance of a flock of pelicans at rest on a large sand bar attached to a small island, the number of which would, if estimated, appear almost incredible. They appeared to cover several acres of ground.

Lewis, August 8, 1804

The mosquitoes at night were worse than I ever experienced.

Gass, August 11, 1804

Captain Lewis shot a pelican. The bag that it carried its drink contained 5 gallons of water by measure. After we passed the pelican island, there were better than 5 or 6,000 of them flying. They kept before us one day. We rowed 19 miles.

Whitehouse, August 8, 1804

The mosquitoes are very troublesome, and there are a great number of herons this evening.

Clark, August 11, 1804

August 10, 1804, mile 800

We dispatched George Drouillard, R. Fields, Wm. Bratton, and Wm. Labiche back after the deserter Reed with orders if he did not give up peaceably to put him to death, to go to the Oto Village and inquire for La Liberté and bring him to the Omaha village. They had with them a speech on the occasion to the Otos and Missouris, directing a few of their chiefs to come to the Omahas, we would make a peace between them and the Omahas and Sioux; a string of wampum; and a carrot of tobacco. We proceeded on and camped on the starboard side.

Clark, August 7, 1804

Established in about 1854, Decatur, Nebraska is one of the oldest towns in the state.

Pirates of the Missouri River

The Omahas began the practice of river piracy on the Missouri in northern Nebraska. They plundered or extorted goods from St. Louis traders passing through their territory. Chief Blackbird was a notorious thug and pirate who used arsenic to poison those in his tribe who opposed him. In 1802, smallpox killed Blackbird along with a large number of the Omahas. He was buried at Blackbird Hill, now in Iowa, a few miles north of Decatur.

August 13, 1804, mile 859

In this area a Spanish trader Ja. Mackey had a "small fort" in which he traded with the Omahas during the winter of 1795-1796. He called it Fort Charles, after the King of Spain. Some industrial plants now continue Mackey's tradition of trade on the river south of Sioux City, Iowa.

Captain Lewis, myself, and 10 men ascended the hill on the larboard side to the top of a high point where the Omaha King Blackbird was buried 4 years ago. A mound of earth about 12 feet in diameter at the base and 6 feet high is raised over him turfed, and a pole 8 feet high in the center. On this pole is fixed a white flag bound with red, blue, and white. This hill is about 300 feet above the water forming a bluff between that and the water if various height from 40 to 150 feet in height, yellow soft sandstone. From the top of this knoll the river may be seen meandering for 60 or 70 miles.

Clark, August 11, 1804

A prairie wolf came near the bank and barked at us this evening. We made an attempt but could not get him. This animal barks like a large feisty dog. Beaver are very plentiful on this part of the river.

Clark, August 12, 1804

The river channel is much narrower and straighter than it was in 1804. Here, 12 miles south of Sioux City, the Missouri river was ¼ to ½ mile wide.

August 13, 1804, mile 853

We sent a man back or I may say across the bend of the river to step off this distance. He made it 974 yards across. The distance around the bend is 18¾ miles. About 4 miles above the bend is the commencement of a bluff which is about 4 miles long extending on the river, of yellow and brown clay. In some parts in it near the river, a soft sandstone is embedded on the top (which is from 20 to 150 feet above the water, and rises back).

Clark, August 12, 1804

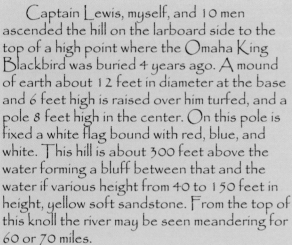

The men sent to the Omaha town last evening have not returned. We concluded to send a spy to know the cause of their delay. At about 12 o'clock the party returned and informed us that they could not find the Indians, nor any fresh sign. Those people have not returned from their buffalo hunt. Those people having no houses, no corn, or anything more than the graves of their ancestors to attach them to the old village, continue in pursuit of the Buffalo longer than others who have greater attachments to their native village.

The ravages of the smallpox (which swept off 400 men, women and children in proportion) has reduced this nation to not exceeding 300 men and left them to the insults of their weaker neighbors, which before were glad to be on friendly terms with them. I am told when this fatal malady was among them they carried their frenzy to very extraordinary lengths, not only of burning their village, but they put their wives and children to death with a view of their all going together to some better country. They bury their dead on the top of high hills and raise mounds on the top of them. The cause or way those people took the small pox is uncertain. The most probable, from some other nation by means of a war party.

Clark, August 14, 1804

I went with 10 men to a creek dammed by the beavers about half way to the village. With some small willows and bark we made a drag, hauled up the creek, and caught 318 fish of different kinds, i.e. pike, bass, salmon, perch, red horse, small cat, and a kind of perch called silver fish on the Ohio. I caught a shrimp precisely of the shape, size, and flavor of those about New Orleans and the lower part of the Mississippi.

In my absence Captain Lewis sent Mr. Durione, the Sioux interpreter, and three men to examine a fire which threw up an immense smoke from the prairies on the NE side of the river and at no great distance from camp. The object of this party was to find some bands of Sioux, which the interpreter thought were near the smoke, and get them to come in. In the evening this party returned and informed that the fire arose from some trees which had been left burning by a small party of Sioux who had passed several days ago. The wind setting from that point blew the smoke from that point over our camp. Our party is all in health and spirits. The men sent to the Otos and in pursuit of the deserter Reed have not yet returned or joined our party.

Clark, August 15, 1804

Captain Lewis took 12 men and went to the pond and creek between camp and the old village, and caught upwards of 800 fine fish. There were 79 pike, 8 fish resembling salmon and trout, 1 rock, 1 flat back, 128 buffalo and red horse, 4 bass, 490 cats, and several small silver fish and shrimp. I had a mast made and fixed to the boat today.

Clark, August 16, 1804

The Neal 4 Power Plant south
of Sioux City receives coal
from Wyoming by rail.

August 13, 1804, mile 861

The expedition caught more than 1,000 fish in two days, about a
mile and a half up Omaha Creek, across the river from this plant.

August 13, 1804, mile 861

August 20, 1804, mile 873

We landed at the Sioux City Airport, about 4 miles north of the expedition's August 13-19 camp. The tower controller was surprised to see us land and stop short enough to exit the runway on the red taxiway at the left.

The party with the Indians arrived. We met them under a shade near the boat and after a short talk we gave them provisions to eat and proceeded to the trial of Reed. He confessed that he "deserted and stole a public rifle, shot pouch, powder, and ball" and requested we would be as favorable with him as we could consistently with our oaths — which we were and only sentenced him to run the gauntlet four times through the party, and that each man with 9 switches should punish him, and for him not to be considered in future as one of the party. The three principal chiefs petitioned for pardon for this man. After we explained the injury such men could do them by false representations, and explaining the customs of our country, they were all satisfied with the propriety of the sentence and was witness to the punishment.

Captain Lewis's birthday this evening was closed with an extra gill of whiskey and a dance until 11 o'clock.

Clark, August 18, 1804

At 6 o'clock this evening Labiche, one of the party sent to the Otos, joined and informed that the party was behind with one of the deserters, M. B. Reed, and the 3 principal chiefs of the nations. La Liberté they caught but he deceived them and got away. The object of those chiefs coming forward is to make a peace with the Omahas through us. As the Omahas are not at home, this great object cannot be accomplished at this time. We set the prairies on fire to bring the Omahas and Sioux if any were near, this being the usual signal.

Clark, August 17, 1804

August 20, 1804, mile 873

We departed Sioux City just before this Air National Guard F-16.

In this view of Sioux City, the Missouri River is in the foreground and the Floyd River on the right. A monument to Charles Floyd is just to the right (south) of the Floyd River, where he was buried. Erected in 1960, it is the first Historic Landmark registered by the U.S. Government. He was the only member of the expedition to die during the journey.

August 20, 1804, mile 876

The main Oto chief breakfasted with us and begged for a sun glass [magnifying glass]. Those people are all naked, covered only with breech cloths, blankets, or buffalo robes, the flesh side painted of different colors and figures. We showed them many curiosities and the air gun, which they were much astonished at. Those people begged much for whiskey.

Sergeant Floyd is taken very bad all at once with a bilious colic. We attempt to relieve him without success as yet. He gets worst and we are much alarmed at his situation. All attention is to him.

Clark, August 19, 1804

Sergeant Floyd was as bad as he could be, no pulse, and nothing would stay a moment in his stomach or bowels. We passed two islands on the starboard side and at the first bluff on the starboard side, Sergeant Floyd died with a great deal of composure. Before his death he said to me, "I am going away. I want you to write me a letter."

We buried him on the top of the bluff ½ mile below a small river to which we gave his name. He was buried with the honors of war, much lamented. A cedar post with the name "Sergeant C. Floyd died here 20th of August, 1804" was fixed at the head of his grave. This man at all times gave us proofs of his firmness and determined resolution to do service to his country and honor himself. After paying all the honor to our deceased brother, we camped in the mouth of Floyd's River, about 30 yards wide. A beautiful evening.

Clark, August 20, 1804

August 20, 1804, mile 877

Interstate 129 crosses the Missouri River at Sioux City.

These two white specs are boats speeding up the river north of Sioux City.

At 3 miles we landed at a bluff where the two men sent with the horses were waiting with two deer. By examination this bluff contained alum, copperas, cobalt, pyrites, an alum rock soft, and sandstone. Captain Lewis in proving the quality of those minerals was near poisoning himself by the fumes and taste of the cobalt, which had the appearance of soft isinglass. Copperas and alum are very poisonous. Captain Lewis took a dose of salts to work off the effects of the arsenic.

We ordered a vote for Sergeant to choose one of three which may be the highest number [One of Gass, Bratton, and Gibson was to be selected for Floyd's replacement]. Patrick Gass had nineteen votes.

Clark, August 22, 1804

August 21, 1804, mile 897

This part of the Missouri is near the upper end of the Corps of Engineers bank stabilization and navigation work. Above here, at least until the first dam, the river is in a more natural state similar to that seen by Lewis and Clark.

Oct 15, 1804, 1488 mi.

Oct 14, 1804, 1478 mi.

Oct 13, 1804, 1464 mi.

Ashley

Ellendale

Oct 12, 1804, 1446 mi.

Oct 11, 1804, 1439 mi.

Eureka

Britton

Oct 8-10, 1804, 1435 mi.

Oct 7, 1804, 1422 mi.

Mobridge

Sisseton

Proceeding On...
Across South Dakota

Oct 4, 1804, 1369 mi.

Oct 6, 1804, 1403 mi.

Oct 5, 1804, 1388 mi.

Oct 2, 1804, 1348 mi.

Gettysburg

Watertown

Oct 1, 1804, 1336 mi.

Oct 3, 1804, 1356 mi.

Redfield

Clark

Clear Lake

Sep 30, 1804, 1321 mi.

- ● Lewis and Clark Campsite
- ─ Lewis and Clark's Route

Sep 29, 1804, 1300 mi.

Sep 23, 1804, 126

Oahe Dam   Pierre

Fort Pierre

Sep 23, 1804, 126

De Smet

Huron

Volga

Brookings

Sep 22, 1804, 1244 mi.

Sep 21, 1804, 1228 mi.

Fort Thompson

Wessington Springs

Flandreau

Big Bend Dam

Howard

Madison

Dell Rapids

Sep 18, 1804, 1160 mi.

Chamberlain

Sep 15, 1804, 1152 mi.

Sep 16-17, 1804, 1153 mi.

Sep 14, 1804, 1143 mi.

Sep 13, 1804, 1135 mi.

Mitchell

Salem

Hartford

Sioux Falls

South Dakota

Sep 12, 1804, 1123 mi.

Platte

Parkston

Freeman

Lennox

Canton

Rock Ra

Ge

Winner

Gregory

Rosebud

Missouri River

Sep 9, 1804, 1083 mi.

Rock Valley Hu

Sioux Ce

I-29

Beresford

Hawarden

Akron

Le N

Sep 8, 1804, 1069 mi.

Fort Randall Dam

Tyndall

Sep 2, 1804, 1000 mi.

Yankton

Aug 26, 1804, 960 mi.

Aug 25, 1804, 950 mi.

Vermillion

Elk Point

Iowa

Sep 7, 1804, 1051 mi.

Sep 6, 1804, 1046 mi.

Sep 5, 1804, 1037 mi.

Sep 4, 1804, 1024 mi.

Sep 1, 1804, 997 mi.

973 mi.

Gavins
Point Dam

Aug 27,

Aug 24, 1804, 944 mi.

Aug 23, 1804, 932 mi.

Aug 22, 1804, 922 mi.

Nebraska

Aug 21, 1804, 904 mi.

Aug 20, 1804, 879 mi.

Sioux City

Mo

0   25   50 Miles

**Lewis and Clark continued up the Missouri River through
South Dakota from August 20 to October 13, 1804.**

The Vermillion/Newcastle Bridge was completed in 2001, near Lewis and Clark's campsite of August 23, 1804.

We proceeded on past a cliff of white and blue or dark earth of 2 miles in extent on the larboard side, and camped on a sand bar opposite the old village called Petite Arc.
Clark, August 26, 1804

August 24, 1804, mile 933

I walked on shore and killed a fat buck. J. Fields was sent out to hunt. He came to the boat and informed us that he had killed a buffalo in the plain ahead. Captain Lewis took 12 men and had the buffalo brought to the boat in the next bend to the starboard side. Several prairie wolves were seen today. We saw elk standing on the sand bar. The wind blew hard and raised the sands off the bar in such clouds that we could scarcely see. This sand being fine and very light stuck to everything it touched, and in the plain for a half a mile, the distance I was out, every spire of grass was covered with sand or dirt.
Clark, August 23, 1804

August 26, 1804, mile 952

These cliffs are probably of the same formations seen by Clark, if not the same cliffs.

August 24, 1804, mile 934

A few miles above Sioux City, the Missouri becomes wider and shallower with sandbars and snags. Lewis and Clark's Missouri may have resembled this most of the way from Omaha. This part of the river is across from the "Ionia Volcano," later named that after the town Ionia. A few miles to the north is Spirit Mound, called Mountain of Little People by the Indians.

August 24, 1804, mile 935

In a northerly direction from the mouth of this creek in an immense plain a high hill is situated, and appears of a conic form. By the different nations of Indians in this quarter, it is supposed to be the residence of Devils, that they are in human form with remarkable large heads, about 18 Inches high, that they are very watchful, and are armed with sharp arrows with which they can kill at a great distance. They are said to kill all persons who are so hardy as to attempt to approach the hill. They state that tradition informs them that many Indians have suffered by these little people, and among others three Omaha men fell a sacrifice to their merciless fury not many years since. So much do the Omahas, Sioux, Otos, and other neighboring nations believe this fable that no Consideration is sufficient to induce them to approach the hill.

Clark, August 24, 1804

The Ionia Volcano was theorized to generate heat through the decomposition of iron pyrite in damp shales. The chemical reactions generated enough heat to cause steam to rise from the bluff, and even fused some of the sand and clay. Much if not all of the "volcano" has washed into the river, and it no longer generates steam.

August 24, 1804, mile 936

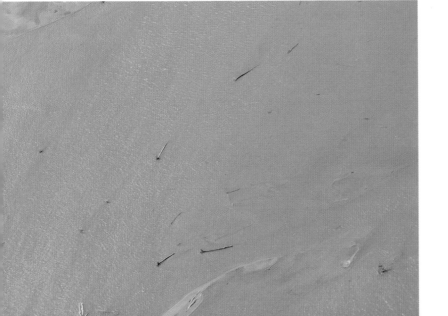

We set out at the usual time and proceeded on the course of last night, to the commencement of a blue clay bluff of 180 or 190 feet high on the larboard side. Those bluffs appear to have been lately on fire, and at this time are too hot for a man to bear his hand on the earth at any depth. There is a great appearance of coal. An immense quantity of cobalt or crystallized substance which answers its description is on the face of the bluff.

Clark, August 24, 1804

Captain Lewis and myself concluded to go and see the mound which was viewed with such terror by all the different nations in this quarter. We selected nine men to go along. From the top of this high land the country is level and open as far as can be seen, except some few rises at a great distance, and the mound which the Indians call Mountain of Little People or Spirits. At 12 o'clock we arrived at the hill. Captain Lewis was much fatigued from heat, the day being very hot and he being in a debilitated state from the precautions he was obliged to take to prevent the effects of the cobalt, and the many substances which had like to have poisoned him two days ago.

The base of the mound is a regular parallelogram, the long side of which is about 300 yards in length, the shorter 60 or 70 yards. From the longer side of the base it rises from the north and south with a steep ascent to the height of 65 or 70 feet, leaving a level plain on the top of 12 feet in width and 90 in length.

The regular form of this hill would in some measure justify a belief that it owed its origin to the hand of man, but as the earth and loose pebbles and other substances of which it was composed it bore an exact resemblance to the steep ground which borders on the creek in its neighborhood, we concluded it was most probably the production of nature.

The only remarkable characteristic of this hill, admitting it to be a natural production, is that it is insulated or separated a considerable distance from any other, which is very unusual in the natural order or disposition of the hills.

From the top of this mound we beheld a most beautiful landscape. Numerous herds of buffalo were seen feeding in various directions. The plain to the north, northwest, and northeast extends without interruption as far as can be seen.

We set the prairies on fire as a signal for the Sioux to come to the river.

Clark, August 25, 1804

August 27, 1804, mile 963

The Lewis and Clark Expedition had deer and elk jerky in this locale. We had green Pringles.

August 27, 1804, mile 962

August 27, 1804, mile 962

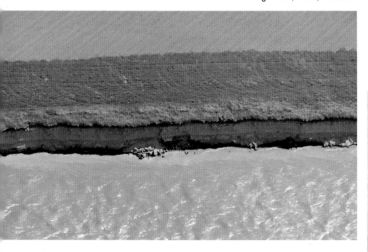

Near this farm, Lewis and Clark camped opposite an abandoned Indian Village called Little Bow, or Petite Arc.

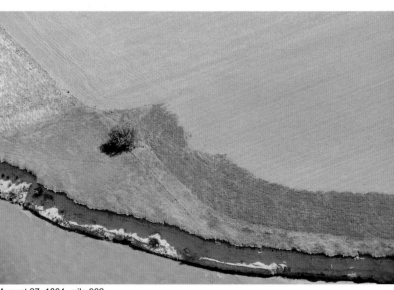

August 27, 1804, mile 962

This village was built by an Indian chief of the Omaha nation by the name of Little Bow. Displeased with the great chief of that nation, Black Bird, he separated with 200 men and built a village at this place. After his death the two villages joined.

Clark, August 26, 1804

This two-level bridge at Yankton, South Dakota has a section that can be raised to provide passage for tall boats.

Lewis and Clark spent three days with five Sioux chiefs and about 70 men and boys near Yankton.

August 28, 1804, mile 978

September 1, 1804, mile 985

As soon as it was dark, a fire was made and a drum was repaired among them. The young men painted themselves different ways, some with their faces all white and others with their faces part white around their foreheads, etc. Then they commenced dancing in a curious manner to us.

There was a party that sung and kept time with the drum. They all danced, or all their young men, especially. They gave a whoop before they commenced dancing. Then they would dance around the fire for some time, then whoop, and then rest a few minutes. One of the warriors would get up in the center with his arms, point toward the different nations, and make a speech, telling what he had done, how many he had killed, how many horses he had stolen, etc. All this makes them great men and fine warriors. The larger rogues are the best men or the bravest men, and those that kill the most get the greatest honor among them.

Whitehouse, August 30, 1804

When the wind was favorable and the mast was not broken, Lewis and Clark made use of a sail on their keelboat and pirogues. The mast occasionally snapped due to high winds or overhanging trees. Here, a windsurfer makes good use of a sail on Lewis and Clark Lake.

The Gavins Point Dam forms Lewis and Clark Lake near Yankton, South Dakota.

August 28, 1804, mile 982

Great numbers of catfish were caught. Those fish are so plentiful that we catch them at any time and place in the river.

Clark, September 1, 1804

Today's Missouri River travels roughly 800 miles through North and South Dakota. From here to the Montana border, more than three quarters of that length is made up of five large reservoirs:

Lewis and Clark Lake	25 miles
Lake Francis Case	107 miles
Lake Sharpe	80 miles
Lake Oahe	231 miles
Lake Sakakawea	178 miles

We passed high bluffs on the south side, and high prairie land on the north. On the north side, the hills come close to the river, and are so near on both sides as not to be more than two miles from each other.

Gass, September 1, 1804

September 3, 1804, mile 1001

We proceeded on past the island and landed on the starboard side above under a yellow clay bluff of 110 feet high.

Clark, September 2, 1804

September 2, 1804, mile 1000

This yellow clay bluff along the starboard side of Lewis and Clark Lake is no longer 110 feet high, since Gavins Point Dam has raised the water level substantially.

The upper end of Lewis and Clark Lake is a marshy area. The dams above this point in the river control flooding and allow grass to grow on the numerous sand bars that Lewis and Clark encountered.

The bluffs in the distance are those below the mouth of Plum Creek.

September 3, 1804, mile 1008

September 3, 1804, mile 1009

We set out at sunrise and proceeded on to a bluff below the mouth of Plum Creek on the starboard side and took an observation of the sun's altitude. This creek is small and abounds with plums of a delicious flavor. The river is wide and crowded with sandbars.

Clark, September 3, 1804

September 3, 1804, mile 1015

September 4, 1804, mile 1021

Chief Standing Bear Memorial Bridge, completed in 1998, crosses the Missouri near Niobria, Nebraska.

The wind shifted to the south and blew very hard. We hoisted the sail and ran very fast a short time, then broke our mast.

Ordway, September 4, 1804

September 4, 1804, mile 1019

This retired boat is near the mouth of the River au Platte, now called Bazile Creek.

The Ponca River comes into the Missouri from the west. This river is about 30 yards wide. We dispatched two men to the Ponca village situated in a handsome plain on the lower side of this creek about 2 miles from the Missouri.

Clark, September 5, 1804

September 5, 1804, mile 1032

Development has come to the Missouri River banks near the mouth of the Ponca River.

September 5, 1804, mile 1030

I saw several goats [antelope] on the hills on the starboard side, also buffalo in great numbers.

Clark, September 6, 1804

September 5, 1804, mile 1031

On the starboard side passed under a bluff of blue earth, under which several mineral springs broke out the water of which had a taste like salts. We came to on the upper point of a large island. Here we made a cedar mast.

Clark, September 5, 1804

September 6, 1804, mile 1043

September 6, 1804, mile 1043

Many of the bluffs in this area exhibit interesting colors.

We landed near the foot of a round mountain, which I saw yesterday, resembling a dome [known as "the tower," in Boyd County, Nebraska]. Captain Lewis and myself walked up to the top which forms a cone and is about 70 feet higher than the high lands around it. The base is about 300 feet. In descending this cupola, we discovered a village of small animals that burrow in the ground. Those animals are called by the French *petite chien*. We killed one and caught one alive by pouring a great quantity of water into his hole. We attempted to dig to the beds of one of those animals.

After digging 6 feet, we found by running a pole down that we were not half way to his lodge. We found two frogs in the hole, and killed a dark rattlesnake near with a ground rat [prairie dog] in him. Those rats are numerous. The village of those animals covers about 4 acres of ground on a gradual descent of a hill and contains great numbers of holes on the top of which those little animals set erect make a whistling noise and when alarmed, step into their hole. We poured into one of the holes five barrels of water without filling it.

Those animals are about the size of a small squirrel, shorter and thicker, the head much resembling a squirrel in every respect except the ears, which are shorter. Their tail is like a ground squirrel which they shake and whistle when alarmed. Their toenails are long. They have fine fur and the longer hairs are gray.

Clark, September 7, 1804

September 6, 1804, mile 1039

The Missouri forms the border between Nebraska, on the left, and South Dakota, on the right.

Fishing is still fruitful along the Missouri River in South Dakota.

September 5, 1804, mile 1032

September 6, 1804, mile 1040

We got fast several times on the sandbars.
Ordway, September 6, 1804

September 6, 1804, mile 1046

Making hay along the Missouri.

September 8, 1804, mile 1055

September 8, 1804, mile 1055

We passed the house of Truteau where he wintered in 1796, called the Pawnee House.

Clark, September 8, 1804

I went out with one of our men who had killed a buffalo and left his hat to keep off the vermin and beasts of prey, but when we came to the place, we found the wolves had devoured the carcass and carried off the hat. Here we found a white wolf dead, supposed to have been killed in a contest for the buffalo.

Gass, September 8, 1804

The Fort Randall Dam and Lake Francis Case are just above Truteau's Pawnee House. Jean Baptiste Truteau was a schoolmaster in St. Louis at the time of the Lewis and Clark expedition. In 1794 he led a Spanish expedition in an attempt to reach the Mandan villages, but they were turned back by the Sioux and spent the winter here. In 1795 he said that he had been making trips into Indian country for 26 years. September 8, 1804, mile 1058

This speeding fisherman spotted an unusual airplane, while his partner seemed intent on holding onto his hat.

September 8, 1804, mile 1060

September 10, 1804, mile 1090

On a hill on the larboard side we found the backbone of a fish, 45 feet long tapering to the tail. There were some teeth, etc. The joints were separated and all was petrified.

Clark, September 10, 1804

I saw at one view 500 buffalo. Those animals have been in view all day feeding in the plains on the larboard side. Every copse of timber appears to have elk or deer. Drouillard killed 3 deer, I killed a buffalo, York 2, R. Fields 1.

Clark, September 9, 1804

Here was the man who left us with the horses 16 days ago (George Shannon. He started August 26.) and has been ahead ever since, joined us nearly starved to death. He had been 12 days without anything to eat but grapes and one rabbit, which he killed by shooting a piece of hard stick in place of a ball. This man, supposing the boat to be ahead, pushed on as long as he could. When he became weak and feeble he determined to lay by and wait for a trading boat, which is expected, keeping one horse for the last resource. Thus a man had like to have starved to death in a land of plenty for want of bullets or something to kill his meat.

Clark, September 11, 1804

September 11, 1804, mile 1108

The Platte-Winner Bridge spans Lake Francis Case near the place the expedition found George Shannon, who had been lost for several days.

September 14, 1804, mile 1136

An old South Dakota church.

Vast herds of buffalo, deer, elk, and antelope were seen feeding in every direction as far as the eye of the observer could see.

Lewis, September 16, 1804

I do not think to exaggerate when I estimate the number of buffalo which could be comprehended at one view to amount to 3,000.

Lewis, September 17, 1804

I walked on shore and saw goats, elk, buffalo, black tail deer, and the common deer. I killed one prairie wolf [coyote], about the size of a gray fox, bushy tail, head and ears like a wolf, and some fur. They burrow in the ground and bark like a small dog. What has been taken heretofore for the fox was those wolves, and no foxes have been seen. The large wolves [gray wolves] are very numerous. They are a light color, large, and have long hair with coarse fur.

Clark, September 18, 1804

September 13, 1804, mile 1126

Windbreaks surround many farms in South Dakota. However, we were not sure whether this windbreak ever had a farm.

The Big Bend Dam forms Lake Sharpe at what the French called the Grand Detour. Clark noted that the river made a 30-mile bend that could be avoided by walking 2,000 yards.

The "Grand Detour" today.

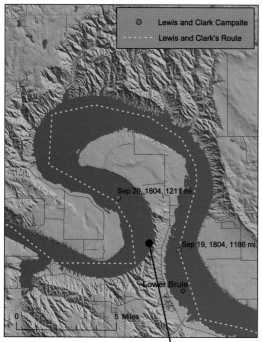

Legend:
○ Lewis and Clark Campsite
····· Lewis and Clark's Route

Sep 20, 1804, 1211 mi.
Sep 19, 1804, 1186 mi.
Lower Brule
0   5 Miles

The irregular hills of the Grand Detour made it easier to follow the river than to portage a half mile across the bend.

September 19, 1804, mile 1175

At half past one o'clock this morning the sand bar on which we camped began to undermine and give way, which alarmed the sergeant of the guard. The motion of the boat awakened me. I got up and by the light of the moon observed that the sand have given way both above and below our camp and was falling in fast.

I ordered all hands on as quick as possible and pushed off. We had pushed off but a few minutes before the bank under which the boat and pirogues lay gave way, which would certainly have sunk both pirogues. By the time we made the opposite shore our camp fell in. We made a second camp for the remainder of the night.

Clark, September 21, 1804

September 21, 1804, mile 1216

I walked on shore with a view of examining this bend. I crossed at the narrowest part, which is high, irregular hills of about 180 or 190 feet. This place the gauge of the bend is 1 miles and a quarter (from river to river or across). From this high land which is only in the gauge, the bend is a beautiful plain through which I walked. I saw numbers of buffalo and goats [antelope].

Clark, September 20, 1804

Our hunters joined us after having killed 2 deer and a beaver. They complain much of the mineral substances in the barren hills over which they passed destroying their moccasins.

Clark, September 22, 1804

We passed an old Indian camp where we found some of their dog-poles, which answer for setting poles. The reason they are called dog-poles is because the Indians fasten their dogs to them and make them draw them from one camp to another loaded with skins and other articles.

Gass, September 22, 1804

A view up Lake Sharpe, to the west.

September 23, 1804, mile 1248

The South Dakota State Capitol faces the Missouri River at Pierre.

September 25, 1804, mile 1278

The [Sioux] squaws are cheerful, fine looking women, not handsome, high cheeks, dressed in skins, a petticoat and robe which folds back over their shoulder with long wool. They do all their laborious work and I may say are perfect slaves to the men, as all squaws of nations much at war, or where the women are more numerous than the men.

Those people have some brave men which they make use of as soldiers. Those men attend to the police of the village and correct all errors. I saw one of them today whip two squaws, who appeared to have fallen out. When he approached, all about appeared to flee with great terror.

Clark, September 26, 1804

Three Sioux boys swam the river and came to us, and informed us that the band of Sioux called the Tetons of 80 lodges were camped at the next creek above, and 60 lodges more a short distance above. We gave those boys two carrots of tobacco to carry to their chiefs, with directions to tell them that we would speak with them tomorrow.

Clark, September 23, 1804

A train crosses the river in Pierre, South Dakota.

September 26, 1804, mile 1279

The Indians did not incline to let us go any further up the river. They held the cable of the pirogue and said that they wanted one pirogue at least to stay, as they were poor. Captain Clark insisted on going on board, but they resisted for a long time. They said they had soldiers on shore as well as he had on board. Captain Clark told them that he had men and medicine on board that would kill 20 such nations in one day. They then began to be still, and only wished that we would stop at their lodges until their women and children would see us.

Four of them came on board, and we proceeded 1 mile and anchored out at the lower point of an island in the middle of the river. The four Indians stayed with us all night.

Whitehouse, September 25, 1804

On September 25, 1804, after a potentially dangerous confrontation with the Sioux, the expedition moved upstream from here about a mile and stopped on an island. Clark wrote, "I call this island Bad Humor Island as we were in a bad humor."

September 26, 1804, mile 1279

We set out early and proceeded on four miles. The bank of the river on the south side was covered all the way with Indians. At 10 o'clock we met the whole band, and anchored about 100 yards from the shore. Captain Lewis, the chiefs, and some men went on shore. The Indians were peaceable and kind. After some time, Captain Lewis returned on board and Captain Clark went on shore.

When the Indians saw Captain Clark coming, they met him with a buffalo robe, spread it out, and made him get into it. Then eight of them carried him to the council house. About an hour afterward, some of them came for Captain Lewis, he landed, and eight of them carried him to the council house in the same manner. They killed several dogs for our people to feast on, and spent the greater part of the day in eating and smoking. At night the women assembled, and danced until 11 o'clock. Then the officers came on board with two chiefs, who continued with us until the morning.

Gass, September 26, 1804

Captain Lewis came on shore and we continued until we were sleepy and returned to our boat. The 2nd chief and one principal man accompanied us. Those two Indians accompanied me on board in the small pirogue. Captain Lewis with a guard was still on shore. The man who steered, not being much accustomed to steer, passed the bow of the boat, and the pirogue came broad side against the cable and broke it. This obliged me to order in a loud voice all hands up and at their oars. My preemptory order to the men and the bustle of their getting to their oars alarmed the chiefs, together with the appearance of the men on shore. As the boat turned, the chief holloed and alarmed the camp or town, informing them that the Omahas were about attacking them.

In about 10 minutes the bank was lined with men armed, the 1st chief at their head. About 200 men appeared and after about one hour returned, except about 60 men who continued on the bank all night. The chiefs continued all night with us. This alarm I as well as Captain Lewis considered as the signal of their intentions (which was to stop our proceeding on our journey and, if possible, rob us.) We were on our guard all night.

Clark, September 27, 1804

Oahe Dam forms Lake Oahe, a large reservoir above Pierre, South Dakota. Lewis and Clark spent three days with the Teton Sioux in this area. The expedition's encounters with the Teton Sioux were probably the most serious and potentially hazardous that they had with any tribe on their way to the Pacific. They danced, smoked pipes, and talked, but they also had a few very dangerous confrontations and misunderstandings. There was no bloodshed.

September 28, 1804, mile 1285

With great difficulty we got the chiefs out of our boat, and when we were about setting out, the class called the soldiers took possession of the cable. The 1st chief was still on board, and intended to go a short distance up with us. I told him the men of his nation set on the cable. He went out and told Captain Lewis, who was at the bow, that the men who set on the rope were soldiers and wanted tobacco. Captain Lewis said he would not agree to be forced into anything. The 2nd chief demanded a flag and tobacco, which we refused to give, stating proper reasons to them for it.

After much difficulty, which had nearly reduced us to necessity of hostilities, I threw a carrot of tobacco to the 1st chief and took the port fire from the gunner. I spoke so as to touch his pride. The chief gave the tobacco to his soldiers and he jerked the rope from them and handed it to the bowsman. We then set out under a breeze from the southeast. About 2 miles up we observed the 3rd chief on shore, beckoning to us. We took him on board. He informed us the rope was held by the order of the 2nd chief, who was a double spoken man.

Soon after, we saw a man coming full speed through the plains. He left his horse and proceeded across a sand bar near the shore. We took him on board and observed that he was the son of the chief we had on board. We sent by him a message to the nation stating the cause of our hoisting the red flag under the white. If they were for peace stay at home and do as we had directed them, if they were for war or were determined to stop us, we were ready to defend ourselves. We halted one hour and a half on the starboard side and made a substitute of stones for an anchor, refreshed our men, and proceeded on.

Clark, September 28, 1804

September 28, 1804, mile 1285

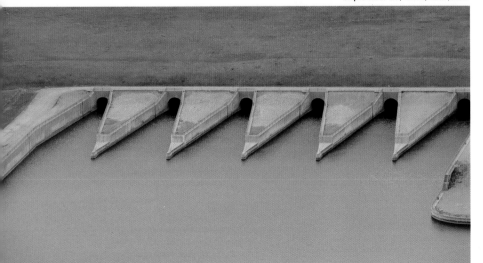

Sandbars are so numerous that it is impossible to describe them, and I think it unnecessary to mention them.

Clark, September 30, 1804

Lake Oahe, South Dakota now covers the river and the sand bars that Lewis and Clark experienced.

September 30, 1804, mile 1308

A short time before night, the waves ran very high and the boat rocked a great deal, which so alarmed our old chief that he would not go any further. We encamped on the north side.

Gass, September 30, 1804

September 29, 1804, mile 1294

September 30, 1804, mile 1307

We are obliged to haul the boat over a sand bar after making several attempts to pass.

Clark, October 1, 1804

We flew over these cattle and thought it an interesting contrast to see cattle in the same area that buffalo dominated 200 years earlier.

September 30, 1804, mile 1319

October 3, 1804, mile 1352

In a few more miles we found this herd of buffalo.

October 2, 1804, mile 1348

We saw brant and
white gulls flying
southerly in large flocks.
Clark, October 3, 1804

October 2, 1804, mile 1343

We spent some time flying the
Lake Oahe shoreline.

We saw a gang of goats
[antelope] swimming across
the river, of which we killed
four. They were not fat.
Clark, October 5, 1804

October 4, 1804, mile 1366

October 4, 1804, mile 1369

October 4, 1804, mile 1369

Lewis and Clark found horses with Indians across the continent, and were sometimes amazed at riding ability of the Indians. Lewis was unable to find out from the Indians whether horses were native to America. We know now that horses were first brought to America by the Europeans.

October 4, 1804, mile 1369

October 5, 1804, mile 1370

The Highway 72 Bridge crosses Lake Oahe near the river called *We Tar Hoo* by the Arikaras. Now it is called Grand River.

We passed a willow mouth of a river called by the Arikaras *We Tar Hoo* on the larboard side. This river is 120 yards wide, the water of which at this time is confined within 20 yards. Great quantities of red berries resembling currants are on the river in every bend.

Clark, October 8, 1804

The Mobridge, South Dakota Municipal Airport is near the expedition's camp of October 7, 1804.

Many large round stones are near the middle of the river. Those stones appear to have been washed from the hills. We passed a village of about 80 neat lodges covered with earth and picketed around. Those lodges are spacious, of an octagon form, as close together as they can possibly be placed, and appear to have been inhabited last spring. From the canoes of skins, mats, buckets, etc. found in the lodges, we are of opinion they were the Arikaras. We found squashes of 3 different kinds growing in the village. One of our men killed an elk close by this village. I saw 2 wolves in pursuit of another, which appeared to be wounded and nearly tired. We proceeded on and found the river shoal.

We made several attempts to find the main channel between the sandbars, and were obliged at length to drag the boat over to save a league, which we must return to get into the deepest channel. We have been obliged to hunt a channel for some time past, the river being divided in many places in a great number of channels. We saw geese, swans, brants, and ducks of different kinds on the sand bars today. Captain Lewis walked on shore and saw great numbers of prairie hens. I observe but few gulls or plover in this part of the river. The corvus or magpie is very common in this quarter.

Clark, October 6, 1804

Two of our men discovered the Arikara village about the center of the island on the larboard side on the main shore. This island is about 3 miles long, separated from the larboard side by a channel of about 60 yards wide and very deep. The island is covered with fields where those people raise their corn, tobacco, beans, etc. Great numbers of those people came on the island to see us pass.

Clark, October 8, 1804

October 14, 1804, mile 1469

Those Indians (Arikaras) were much astonished at my servant. They never saw a black man before. All flocked around him and examined him from top to toe. He carried on the joke and made himself more terrible that we wished him to do. Those Indians are not fond of spirituous liquor of any kind.

Clark, October 10, 1804

There have been farms in North and South Dakota along the Missouri River for hundreds of years. Today's farms are a bit more modern than the ones Lewis and Clark found, although some of today's farmers are likely descendants of those Arikaras that welcomed Lewis and Clark.

October 12, 1804, mile 1444

October 18, 1804, mile 1511

We came to the second village of the Arikaras, situated on a prairie on the south side. They had the American flag hoisted which Captain Lewis gave them yesterday. They are the most cleanly Indians I have ever seen on the voyage, as well as the most friendly and industrious.

Gass, October 11, 1804

A curious custom with the Sioux as well as the Arikaras is to give handsome squaws to those whom they wish to show some acknowledgements to. The Sioux we got clear of without taking their squaws. They followed us with squaws for two days. The Arikaras we put off during the time we were at the towns, but two handsome young squaws were sent by a man to follow us. They came up this evening and persisted in their civilities.

Clark, October 12, 1804

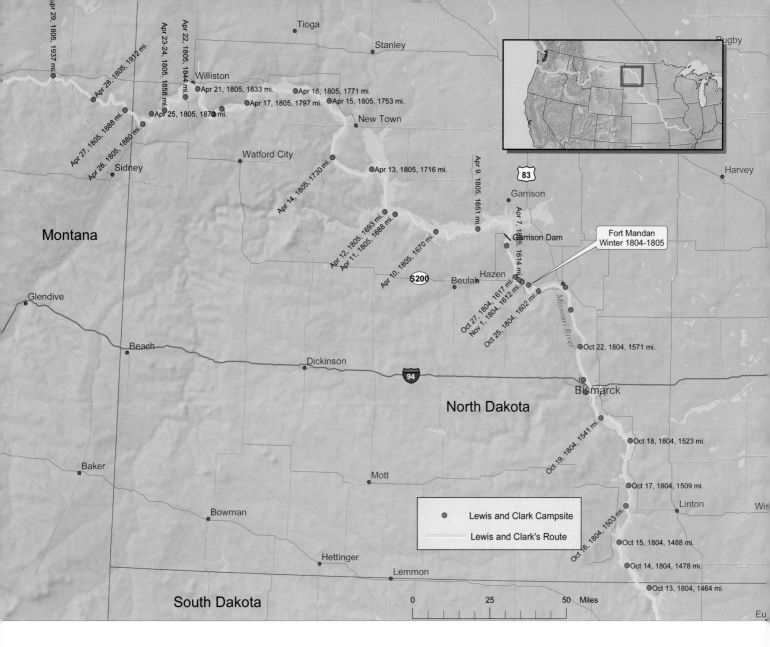

Apr 29, 1805, 1937 mi.

Apr 22, 1805, 1912 mi.
Apr 28, 1805, 1912 mi.
Apr 23-24, 1805, 1844 mi.
Apr 22, 1805, 1858 mi.

Williston
Apr 21, 1805, 1833 mi.
Apr 16, 1805, 1771 mi.

Apr 25, 1805, 1873 mi.
Apr 17, 1805, 1797 mi.
Apr 15, 1805, 1753 mi.

Apr 27, 1805, 1888 mi.

Apr 26, 1805, 1880 mi.
Sidney

New Town

Tioga

Stanley

Rugby

Harvey

Watford City

Apr 13, 1805, 1716 mi.

Apr 9, 1805, 1651 mi.

83

Garrison

Montana

Apr 14, 1805, 1730 mi.

Apr 7, 1805, 1614 mi.

Garrison Dam

Fort Mandan
Winter 1804-1805

Apr 12, 1805, 1693 mi.
Apr 11, 1805, 1688 mi.

Glendive

Apr 10, 1805, 1670 mi.

S200

Beulah

Hazen

Oct 27, 1804, 1617 mi.
Nov 1, 1804, 1612 mi.
Oct 25, 1804, 1602 mi.

Missouri River

Beach

Oct 22, 1804, 1571 mi.

Dickinson

94

Bismarck

North Dakota

Oct 19, 1804, 1541 mi.

Oct 18, 1804, 1523 mi.

Baker

Mott

Oct 17, 1804, 1509 mi.

Linton

Wis

Bowman

Lewis and Clark Campsite

Lewis and Clark's Route

Oct 16, 1804, 1503 mi.

Oct 15, 1804, 1488 mi.

Hettinger

Lemmon

Oct 14, 1804, 1478 mi.

South Dakota

0   25   50   Miles

Oct 13, 1804, 1464 mi.

Eu

Proceeding On...
Through North Dakota

Lewis and Clark continued up the Missouri River into North Dakota to the
Mandan Indian villages, where they stopped for the winter. The following
April, when the river was clear of ice, they continued their journey.

October 18, 1804, mile 1511

We saw great numbers of goats [antelope] on the shore starboard side. We proceeded on. Captain Lewis and the Indian Chief walked on shore. Soon after, I discovered great numbers of goats in the river, and Indians on the shore of each side. As I approached or got nearer I discovered boys in the water killing the goats with sticks and hauling them to shore. Those on the banks shot them with arrows and as they approached the shore would turn them back. Of this gang of goats I counted 58 of which they had killed on the shore. One of our hunters out with Captain Lewis killed three goats.

We passed the camp on the starboard side, proceeded ½ mile, and camped on the larboard side. Many Indians came to the boat to see. Some came across late at night. As they approach they holloed and sung. After staying a short time, two went for some meat and returned in a short time with fresh dried buffalo, also goat. Those Indians stayed all night. They sung and were very merry the greater part of the night.

Clark, October 16, 1804

Great numbers of goats [antelope] are flocking down to the starboard side of the river, on their way to the Black Mountains where they winter. Those animals return in the spring the same way and scatter in different directions.

Clark, October 17, 1804

We passed a sandstone bluff where we found round stone in the form of cannon balls. Some of them are very large. We took one of them on board to answer for an anchor.

Ordway, October 18, 1804

October 17, 1804, mile 1508

We passed an Indian camp. We halted above and about 30 of the Indians came over in their canoes of skins. We ate with them. They gave us meat. In return we gave fish hooks and some beads. About a mile higher we came to at the camp of the Arikaras of about 8 lodges. We also ate and they gave us some meat. We proceeded on and saw numbers of Indians on both sides passing a creek.

Those people are much pleased with my black servant. Their women are very fond of caressing our men, etc.

Clark, October 15, 1804

We passed several flocks of pelicans between Pierre, South Dakota and Bismarck, North Dakota.

October 20, 1804, mile 1546

At the upper part of Lake Oahe, the Missouri returns to its shallow, meandering style.

October 19, 1804, mile 1526

I walked out on the hill and observed great numbers of buffalo feeding on both sides of the river. I counted 52 gangs of buffalo and 3 of elk at one view. I saw some remarkable round hills forming a cone at the top, one about 90 feet, one 60, and several others smaller. The Indian Chief says that the calumet birds [golden eagles] live in the holes of those hills.

Clark, October 19, 1804

We saw great numbers of buffalo, elk, deer, and goats. Our hunters killed 10 deer and a goat today, and wounded a white bear [grizzly]. I saw several fresh tracks of those animals, which are three times as large as a man's tracks. Great numbers of buffalo were swimming in the river. I observe wolves near all large gangs of buffalo, and when the buffalo move, those animals follow and feed on those that are killed by accident or those that are too pore of fat to keep up with the gang.

Clark, October 20, 1804

The Bismarck Community Bowl, Bismarck's community sports stadium, is next to the Missouri River. Lewis and Clark camped near here on October 20, 1804, the day they had their first encounter with a grizzly bear. There was an abandoned Mandan village in this area when Lewis and Clark arrived. The Indians had moved a few miles upstream after a severe smallpox epidemic.

October 21, 1804, mile 1559

> At 7 o'clock we came to at a camp of Teton Sioux on the larboard side. Those people, 12 in number, were naked (except for their leggings) and had the appearance of war. We have every reason to believe that they were going to or have been to steal horses from the Mandans.
>
> *Clark, October 22, 1804*

October 22, 1804, mile 1561

The Mandan Refinery was built in 1954 just upstream from Bismarck.

A railroad yard separates the Heskett Power Station and the Mandan Refinery, north of Bismarck. Heskett Station was also built in 1954.

October 22, 1804, mile 1565

A lone kayaker heads upstream, outside Bismarck.

October 22, 1804, mile 1565

We have seen no game on the river today, proof of the Indians hunting in the neighborhood.

We saw one of the grand chiefs of the Mandans, with five lodges, hunting. This chief met the chief of the Arikaras who accompanied us with great cordiality and ceremony.

Clark, October 24, 1804

The Missouri riverfront is a popular site for new homes.

October 22, 1804, mile 1565

October 22, 1804, mile 1570

> The river is full of sandbars and we are at a great loss to find the channel of the river. We frequently run on the sandbars, which detains us much.
>
> *Clark, October 25, 1804*

A half-dozen Canadian geese follow the river.

October 23, 1804, mile 1575

This feedlot is a few miles up the river from Bismarck, opposite a sandbar.

The expedition built Fort Mandan and spent an enjoyable winter there among the Mandan and Hidatsa Indians. Fort Mandan was a few miles upstream from Washburn, North Dakota, seen in this photo.

October 24, 1804, mile 1590

Several Indians came to see us this evening, amongst others the son of the late great chief of the Mandans. This man has his two little fingers off. On inquiring the cause, I was told it was customary for this nation to show their grief by some testimony of pain, and that it was not uncommon for them to take off two smaller fingers of the hand and sometimes more with other marks of savage affection.

Clark, October 25, 1804

October 25, 1804, mile 1595

We camped about half a mile below the first Mandan town on the larboard side. Soon after our arrival, many men, women, and children flocked down to see us. Captain Lewis walked to the village with the principal chiefs and our interpreters. I smoked with the chiefs who came after. Those people seemed much pleased with the corn mill, which we were obliged to use and was fixed to the boat.

Clark, October 26, 1804

October 25, 1804, mile 1595

Fort Mandan washed into the Missouri a few years after it was built. A replica of Fort Mandan has been erected north of the original location.

A man chopping wood under the American Flag raised his axe in salute as we flew over. Lewis and Clark raised the American Flag for the first time in Fort Mandan on Christmas Morning, 1804. What appears to be the beginning of a canoe is visible outside the right corner of the fort.

October 25, 1804, mile 1596

After spending the night near the Fort Mandan site, Lewis and Clark went a few miles up river for about a week, near the two Mandan villages. They returned to the site down river where more wood and game was available for the winter. On November 2 they began cutting wood for their winter home, where they stayed until April 6. The original Fort Mandan site is in the distance in this photo.

An iron or steel corn mill which we gave to the Mandans was very thankfully received.

Clark, October 29, 1804

In 1806, Alexander Henry (the younger) visited the Mandans and noted, "I saw the remains of an excellent large corn mill, which the foolish fellows had demolished to barb their arrows. The largest piece of it, which they could not break or work up into any weapon, was fixed to a wooden handle and used to pound marrow bones to make grease."

The prairie was set on fire (or caught by accident) by a young man of the Mandans. The fire went with such velocity that it burned to death a man and woman who could not get to any place of safety. One man, a woman, and a child were much burned and several narrowly escaped the flame. A boy, half white, was saved unhurt in the midst of the flame. Those ignorant people say this boy was saved by the great medicine spirit because he was white. The cause of his being saved was a green buffalo skin thrown over him by his mother who perhaps had more foresight for the protection of her son and less for herself than those who escaped the flame. This fire passed our camp last night about 8 o'clock p.m. It went with great rapidity and looked tremendous.

Clark, October 29, 1804

Thomas Jefferson was re-elected President by the electoral college on December 5, 1804, after more than a month of popular elections in the 17 states. Lewis and Clark probably did not know this until their return in 1806.

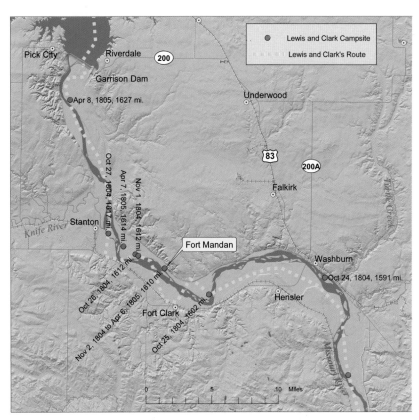

Fort Mandan Area, North Dakota

But few Indians visited us today, the ice having broken up in several places. The ice began to break away this evening, and was near destroying our canoes as they were descending to the fort. The river rose only 9 inches today. We are preparing to depart.

Clark, March 25, 1805

The obstacle broke away above, and the ice came down in great quantities. The river rose 13 inches in the last 24 hours. I observed extraordinary dexterity of the Indians in jumping from one cake of ice to another for the purpose of catching the buffalo as they float down. Many of the cakes of ice which they pass over are not two feet square.

The plains are on fire in view of the fort on both sides of the river. It is said to be common for the Indians to burn the plains near their villages every spring for the benefit of their horses, and to induce the buffalo to come near.

Clark, March 29, 1805

The route up the Missouri as far as Fort Mandan was known to traders, but beyond there was uncharted territory. Lewis and Clark got as much information as possible from the Indians about the country to the west.

Toussaint Charbonneau, his wife Sacagawea, and Baptiste LePage, who were living with the Indians, joined the expedition at Fort Mandan. Charbonneau hired on as an interpreter, and LePage enlisted as a private. Lewis and Clark understood that both of Charbonneau's wives would accompany them, but only Sacagawea ended up going.

On April 7, 1805, the large keel boat left Fort Mandan for St. Louis with journals, maps, scientific specimens, and 13 men. On the same day, Lewis and Clark, Sergeants Gass, Ordway, and Pryor, 23 privates, Drouillard, Charbonneau, Sacagawea and her baby, and Clark's slave York departed Fort Mandan toward the Pacific Ocean.

On April 7, 1805, the Lewis and Clark Expedition left Fort Mandan and resumed their journey to the Pacific. On the same day, Beethoven's Eroica Symphony was first performed in Vienna, Austria.

We flew up the river at 60 miles per hour and more, slow for an airplane but somewhat faster than Lewis and Clark's 10-20 miles per day.

April 8, 1805, mile 1619

> About 5 o'clock in the afternoon, we left Fort Mandan in good spirits. 31 men and 1 woman went up the river, and 13 returned down it in the boat. We had 2 pirogues and 6 canoes.
>
> *Gass, April 7, 1805*

> Entertaining as I do the most confident hope of succeeding in a voyage which had formed a darling project of mine for the last ten years, I could but esteem this moment of my departure as among the most happy of my life. The party are in excellent health and spirits, zealously attached to the enterprise, and anxious to proceed; not a whisper of murmur or discontent to be heard among them, but all act in unison, and with the most perfect harmony.
>
> *Lewis, April 7, 1805*

April 7, 1805, mile 1612

> I walked on shore and visited the Black Cat [the upper Mandan village led by Chief Black Cat], took leave of them after smoking a pipe as is their custom, and then proceeded on slowly by land about 4 miles where I waited the arrival of the party. At 12 o'clock they came up and informed me that one of the small canoes was behind in distress. Captain Clark returned and found she had filled with water and all her loading was wet. We lost half a bag of biscuit and about thirty pounds of powder by this accident. The powder we regard as a serious loss, but we spread it to dry immediately and hope we shall still be enabled to restore the greater part of it.
>
> *Lewis, April 8, 1805*

These two power plants, Leland Olds Station and Stanton Station, were each built in 1966 under separate ownership. They mark the location of the Mandan village led by Chief Big White, named that because of his large size and light colored skin.

Lake Sakakawea is the third largest reservoir in the United States.

April 9, 1805, mile 1639

We stopped at an improvised landing strip near the expedition's April 8 campsite.

April 8, 1805, mile 1626

I saw a mosquito today. Great numbers of brant were flying up the river. We passed a hunting camp of Minetares waiting the return of the antelopes. Great numbers of geese were feeding in the prairies on the young grass.

Clark, April 9, 1805

Garrison Dam forms Lake Sakakawea, named after Charbonneau's wife, Sacagawea. (There is some controversy over the spelling of her name, Sacagawea, Sacajawea, or Sakakawea.) She was Shoshone and lived in the mountains of western Montana until a Hidatsa raiding party captured her in 1801 and brought her to this area. The trader Charbonneau won her and another woman in a bet with the warriors who had captured them. When Charbonneau was hired as interpreter for the expedition, he decided to bring only Sacagawea along. She was about 15 years old at the time and pregnant. She had her child on February 11, before the expedition left Fort Mandan for the Pacific. Her knowledge and guidance turned out to be very helpful to Lewis and Clark.

Garrison Dam is one of the largest earthen dams in the world. The tanks above the power plant are surge tanks used to control pressure fluctuations of the water flowing into the generators.

April 9, 1805, mile 1632

April 9, 1805, mile 1632

The bluffs of the river which we passed today were upwards of a hundred feet high, formed of a mixture of yellow clay and sand. Many horizontal stratas of carbonated wood, having every appearance of pitcoal at a distance, were seen on the face of these bluffs.

Lewis, April 9, 1805

April 9, 1805, mile 1646

April 16, 1805, mile 1760

April 16, 1805, mile 1760

The layers Lewis described as carbonated wood are actually lignite coal. They saw these layers over several days of travel.

We saw some buffalo lying along the shore, which had been drowned by falling through the ice in winter, and lodged on shore by the high water when the river broke up about the first of this month. We saw also many tracks of the white bear [grizzly] of enormous size, along the river shore and about the carcasses of the buffalo, on which I presume they feed.

We have not as yet seen one of these animals, though their tracks are so abundant and recent. The men as well as ourselves are anxious to meet with some of these bears. The Indians give very formidable accounts of the strength and ferocity of this animal, which they never dare to attack but in parties of six, eight, or ten persons; and are even then frequently defeated with the loss of one or more of their party.

Two Minetares were killed during the last winter in an attack on a white bear. This animal is said more frequently to attack a man on meeting with him than to flee from him. When the Indians are about to go in quest of the white bear, previous to their departure they paint themselves and perform all those superstitious rights commonly observed when they are about to make war upon a neighboring nation.

Lewis, April 13, 1805

The country from Fort Mandan to this place is so constantly hunted by the Minetares that there is but little game.

Lewis, April 11, 1805

Highway 23 crosses Lake Sakakawea about 40 miles above the Little Missouri River near New Town, North Dakota.

April 15, 1805, mile 1743

All the streams which head a few miles in the hills discharge water which is black and unfit for use. I can safely say that I have not seen one drop of water fit for use above Fort Mandan except the Knife, Little Missouri, and the Missouri rivers; the other streams being so much impregnated with mineral as to be very disagreeable in its present state.

I saw the remains of several camps of Assiniboines. Near one of those camps and at no great distance from the mouth of the aforesaid creek, in a hollow, I saw a large strong pen made for the purpose of catching the antelope, with wings projecting from it widening from the pen.

Clark, April 15, 1805

April 14, 1805, mile 1726

While we remained at the entrance of the Little Missouri, we saw several pieces of pumice stone floating down that stream, a considerable quantity of which had been lodged against a point of driftwood a little above its entrance.

Lewis, April 14, 1805

This morning was a cloudy morning with high wind. We did not set out until the next day. While we lay here, I went to the hills, which I found very high, much washed by the rain, and without grass. I saw a part of a log quite petrified, and of which good whetstones or hones could be made. I also saw where a hill had been on fire, and pumice stone all around it.

Gass, April 19, 1805

Marshy wetlands form at the upper end of Lake Sakakawea.

We saw immense quantities of game in every direction around us as we passed up the river, consisting of herds of buffalo, elk, and antelopes, with some deer and wolves. Though we continue to see many tracks of the bear, we have seen but very few of them, and those are at a great distance generally running from us. I therefore presume that they are extremely wary and shy, The Indian account of them does not correspond with our experience so far.

Lewis, April 17, 1805

The Missouri River narrows above Lake Sakakawea. Williston, North Dakota is in the distance on the right side of this photo.

April 21, 1805, mile 1821

A short distance below our camp I saw some rafts on the starboard side near which an Indian woman was scaffolded in the Indian form of deposing their dead and fallen down. She was or had been raised about six feet, enclosed in several robes tightly laced around her, with her dog sleighs, her bag of different colored earths, paint, small bones of animals, beaver nails, and several other trinkets, also a blue jay. Her dog was killed and lay near her.

Clark, April 20, 1805

April 22, 1805, mile 1836

We stopped at Williston after a short day of flying because of high winds. Lewis and Clark encountered the same problem 197 years earlier.

The wind blew so hard during the whole of this day that we were unable to move. Notwithstanding that we were sheltered by high timber from the effects of the wind, such was its violence that it caused the waves to rise in such manner as to wet many articles in the small canoes before they could be unloaded.

Lewis, April 24, 1805

Captain Clark, concluding that the wind had detained us, came down the river in search of us. He had killed three black tailed, or mule deer, and a buffalo calf in the course of his ramble.

Lewis, April 23, 1805,
coining the common name "mule deer."

The winds of this country, which blow with some violence almost every day, have become a serious obstruction in our progression onward, as we can't move when the wind is high without great risk. The winds are generally ahead and often too violent to proceed.

Clark, April 23, 1805

April 25, 1805, mile 1868

This oil well is one of several along the Missouri near Williston.

April 26, 1805, mile 1880

The Yellowstone River comes into the Missouri about 20 miles southwest of Williston, North Dakota. Clark and 12 others descended the Yellowstone to this point on their return from the Pacific. This view is to the west.

We came to the mouth of the Jaune [Yellowstone] and halted. I went up the point about 9 miles, where there are the most beautiful, rich plains I ever beheld.

Gass, April 26, 1805

The bed of the Yellowstone River is entirely composed of sand and mud, not a stone of any kind to be seen near its entrance.

Lewis, April 26, 1805

April 26, 1805, mile 1880

After I had completed my observations in the evening I walked down and joined the party at their encampment on the point of land formed by the junction of the rivers. I found them all in good health and much pleased at having arrived at this long wished-for spot, and in order to add in some measure to the general pleasure which seemed to pervade our little community, we ordered a dram to be issued to each person. This soon produced the fiddle, and they spent the evening with much hilarity, singing, and dancing, and seemed as perfectly to forget their past toils as they appeared regardless of those to come.

Lewis, April 26, 1805

April 26, 1805, mile 1880

The view above, to the south, and the view on the left, to the north, show the muddier waters of the Yellowstone flowing into the Missouri.

I determined to encamp on the bank of the Yellowstone River, which made its appearance about 2 miles south of me. The whole face of the country was covered with herds of buffalo, elk, and antelopes. Deer are also abundant, but keep themselves more concealed in the woodland. The buffalo, elk, and antelope are so gentle that we pass near them while feeding, without appearing to excite any alarm among them. When we attract their attention, they frequently approach us more nearly to discover what we are, and in some instances pursue us a considerable distance apparently with that view.

Lewis, April 25, 1805

> The bald eagle is more abundant here than I have ever observed in any part of the country.
>
> *Lewis, April 27, 1805*

> The beavers have cut great quantities of timber. We saw a tree nearly 3 feet in diameter that had been felled by them.
>
> *Lewis, April 28, 1805*

April 27, 1805, mile 1887

April 27, 1805, mile 1886

Fort Union was built by the American Fur Company in 1828 to trade with the Assiniboines, the Crows of the upper Yellowstone, and the Blackfeet from farther up the Missouri. The site became the Fort Union Trading Post National Historic Site in 1966. The reconstruction, southwest of Williston, North Dakota, has been done over the past 20 years.

April 28, 1805, mile 1890

> The bluffs in this part as also below show different stratums of coal or carbonated wood, and colored earths such as dark brown, yellow, a lightish brown, and a dark red.
>
> *Clark, April 28, 1805*

A road and a railroad are at the foot of the bluffs described by Clark.

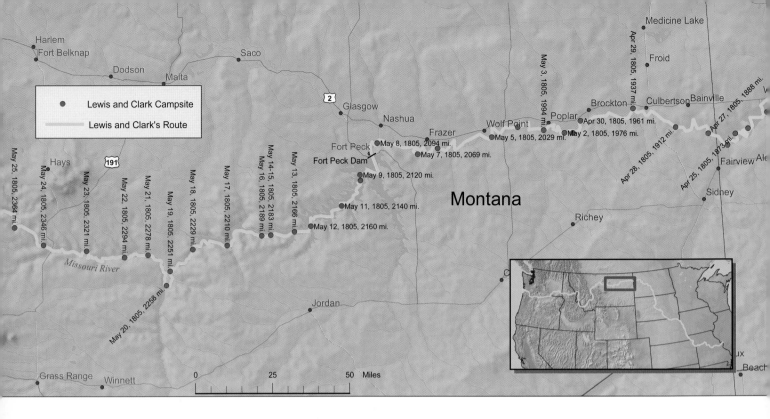

Proceeding On...

Across Eastern Montana

Lewis and Clark arrived in present day Montana on April 27, 1804. They spent almost four months in Montana before they reached Idaho.

Clark saw bighorn sheep on bluffs such as these.

April 28, 1805, mile 1912

We saw a female and her fawn of the bighorn animal on the top of the bluff lying. The noise we made alarmed them and they came down on the side of the bluff which had but little slope being nearly perpendicular. I directed two men to kill those animals. One went on top and the other man near the water. They had two shots at the doe while in motion without effect. Those animals run and skipped about with great ease on this declivity and appeared to prefer it to the level bottom or plain.

Clark, April 29, 1805

About 8 a.m. we fell in with two brown or yellow [grizzly] bears, both of which we wounded. One of them made his escape. The other, after my firing on him, pursued me 70 or 80 yards, but fortunately had been so badly wounded that he was unable to pursue so closely as to prevent my charging my gun. We again repeated our fire and killed him. It was a male not fully grown. We estimated his weight at 300 lbs., not having the means of ascertaining it precisely. It is a much more furious and formidable animal than the black bear, and it will frequently pursue the hunter when wounded. It is astonishing to see the wounds they will bear before they can be put to death.

Lewis, April 29, 1805

April 28, 1805, mile 1907

The Missouri meanders across the country southeast of Culbertson, Montana.

I walked on shore this evening and killed a Deer which was so meager as to be unfit for use. We came to the mouth of a little river on the starboard side which is about 50 or 60 yards from bank to bank. I was up this stream 3 miles. It continues its width and glides with a gentle current. Its water is about 15 yards wide at this time and appears to be navigable for canoes. It meanders through a beautiful and extensive valley as far as can be seen. I saw only a single tree in this fertile valley. The water of this river is clear, of a yellowish color. We call this river Martha's River in honor of the celebrated M.F.

We saw several of the big horn animals this evening. The wolves destroy great numbers of the antelopes by decoying those animals singularly out in the plains and pursuing them alternately. Those antelopes are curious and will approach anything which appears in motion near them.

Clark, April 29, 1805

April 29, 1805, mile 1937

Lewis and Clark camped at the mouth of this river. Clark named it Martha's River, but it is called Big Muddy Creek today. By the time the expedition returned the following year, the mouth of Martha's river had moved downstream on the Missouri about a quarter mile. Today it has moved almost another quarter mile downstream.

The wind blew very hard all last night. This morning about sunrise it began to snow (the thermometer about 28° above zero) and continued until about 10 o'clock, at which time it ceased. The wind continued hard until about 2 p.m. The snow which fell today was about 1 inch deep. It is a very extraordinary climate to behold the trees green and flowers spread on the plain, and snow an inch deep. We set out about 3 o'clock and proceeded on about 5 ½ miles and encamped on the starboard side. The evening was very cold, ice freezing on the oars.

Clark, May 2, 1805

The Missouri takes interesting routes through the plains near Poplar, Montana. Lewis and Clark saw "an unusual number of porcupines" in this area. The river they named the Porcupine is now called the Poplar River.

Near the entrance of the river we saw an unusual number of porcupines, from which we determined to call the river after that animal, and accordingly denominated it Porcupine River. This stream discharges itself into the Missouri on the starboard side 2,000 miles above the mouth of the latter. It is a beautiful bold running stream, 40 yards wide at its entrance. The water is transparent, it being the first of this description that I have yet seen discharge itself into the Missouri. A quarter of a mile above the entrance of this river a large creek falls in which we called 2,000 Mile Creek.

I walked out a little distance and met with two porcupines which were feeding on the young willows which grow in great abundance on all the sandbars. This animal is exceedingly clumsy and not very watchful. I approached so near one of them before it perceived me that I touched it with my spontoon.

Lewis, May 3, 1805

May 4, 1805, mile 2011

I saw immense quantities of buffalo in every direction, also some elk, deer, and goats [antelope]. Having an abundance of meat on hand, I passed them without firing on them. They are extremely gentle. The bull buffalo particularly will scarcely give way to you. I passed several in the open plain within 50 paces. They viewed me for a moment as something novel and then very unconcernedly continued to feed.

Lewis, May 4, 1805

After breakfast I walked on shore and saw great numbers of buffalo and elk. I saw also a den of young wolves and a number of grown wolves in every direction. The country on both sides is as yesterday, handsome and fertile.

Clark, May 5, 1805

May 6, 1805, mile 2049

In this area the Missouri meanders with wide, horseshoe-shaped bends just as it did in 1805.

We saw a brown bear swim the river above us. He disappeared before we could get in reach of him. I find that the curiosity of our party is pretty well satisfied with respect to this animal. The formidable appearance of the male bear killed on the 5th, added to the difficulty with which they die when even shot through the vital parts, has staggered the resolution of several of the men. Others, however, seem keen for action with the bear. I expect these gentlemen will give us some amusement shortly as they soon begin now to copulate.

Lewis, May 6, 1805

May 6, 1805, mile 2033

Captain Clark and Drouillard killed the largest brown bear this evening which we have ever seen. It was a most tremendous looking animal, and extremely hard to kill. Notwithstanding he had five balls through his lungs and five others in various parts, he swam more than half the distance across the river to a sandbar, and it was at least twenty minutes before he died. He did not attempt to attack, but fled and made the most tremendous roaring from the moment he was shot. We had no means of weighing this monster. Captain Clark thought he would weigh 500 lbs. For my own part, I think the estimate too small by 100 lbs. He measured 8 feet 7 ½ inches from the nose to the extremity of the hind feet. He was in good order, we therefore divided him among the party and made them boil the oil and put it in a cask for future use. The oil is hard as hog's lard when cool, much more so than the black bear.

Lewis, May 5, 1805

The muddy water that flows into the Missouri from Hungry Creek is visible for more than 2 miles downstream. The Missouri River water is less muddy below the Fort Peck Dam because much of the suspended sediment settles out in the lake.

May 7, 1805, mile 2067

May 7, 1805, mile 2068

May 7, 1805, mile 2069

We found a train speeding by the Milk River about 4 miles upstream from the Missouri.

The white apple is found in great abundance in this neighborhood. It is confined to the highlands principally. The white apple, so called by the French engages, is a plant which rises to a height of 6 or 9 inches, rarely exceeding a foot. This root forms a considerable article of food with the Indians of the Missouri, who for this purpose prepare them in several ways. They are esteemed good at all seasons of the year but are best from the middle of July to the latter end of autumn, when they are sought and gathered by the provident part of the natives for their winter stores.

Lewis, May 8, 1805

We nooned it just above the entrance of a large river which disembogues on the starboard side. I took advantage of this leisure moment and examined the river about 3 miles. I found it generally 150 yards wide, and in some places 200. It is deep, gentle in its current, and affords a large body of water. Its banks, which are formed of a dark rich loam and blue clay, are abrupt and about 12 feet high. The water of this river possesses a peculiar whiteness, being about the color of a cup of tea with the admixture of a tablespoonful of milk. From the color of its water we call it Milk River.

Lewis, May 8, 1805

The lower Milk River has a lot of bends and nearly doubles back on itself in several places. It was named the Milk River because of its light color. The white apple Lewis describes is the breadroot scurf pea, or prairie turnip.

The Glasgow, Montana airport shows signs of the much larger Glasgow Air Force Base that was active from 1942 to the 1960's. Bomber crews from B-17's to B-52's have trained here.

May 8, 1805, mile 2087

The Missouri keeps its width, which is nearly as wide as near its mouth. There are a great number of sandbars, the water not so muddy, and sand finer and in smaller proportion.
Clark, May 9, 1805

We saw a great quantity of game today, particularly of Elk and buffalo. The latter are now so gentle that the men frequently throw sticks and stones at them in order to drive them out of the way. We also saw this evening immense quantities of timber cut by the beaver which appeared to have been done the preceding years. In one place particularly they had cut all the timber down for three acres in front and on nearly one back from the river, and had removed a considerable proportion of it. The timber grew very thick and some of it was as large as a man's body.
Lewis, May 9, 1805

May 9, 1805, mile 2102

Today we passed the bed of the most extraordinary river that I ever beheld. It is as wide as the Missouri is at this place, or ½ mile wide, and not containing a single drop of running water, some small standing pools being all the water that could be perceived. I walked up this river about 3 miles and ascended an eminence from which I could perceive it many miles.
Lewis, May 9, 1805

The 250-foot high Fort Peck Dam was completed in 1938. It was completed again in 1940. On September 22, 1938, just two weeks after its completion, 5 million cubic yards of earth from the new dam slid into the Missouri River. Eight people were killed. The dam was rebuilt with a wider base and other improvements.

The dry river that Lewis described is now the Big Dry Arm of Fort Peck Lake, fed by Big Dry Creek.

In the evening the men in two of the rear canoes discovered a large brown bear lying in the open grounds about 300 paces from the river, and six of them went out to attack him, all good hunters. They took the advantage of a small eminence which concealed them and got within 40 paces of him unperceived. Two of them reserved their fires as had been previously concerted. The four others fired nearly at the same time and put each his bullet through the bear. Two of the balls passed through the bulk of both lobes of his lungs. In an instant this monster ran at them with open mouth. The two who had reserved their fires discharged their pieces at him as he came towards them. Both of them struck him, one only slightly and the other fortunately broke his shoulder. This, however, retarded his motion for a moment only.

The men, unable to reload their guns, took flight. The bear pursued and had very nearly overtaken them before they reached the river. Two of the party betook themselves to a canoe, and the others separated and concealed themselves among the willows, reloaded their pieces, and each discharged his piece at him as they had an opportunity. They struck him several times again, but the guns served only to direct the bear to them.

In this manner he pursued two of them separately so close that they were obliged to throw aside their guns and pouches and throw themselves into the river, although the bank was nearly 20 feet perpendicular. So enraged was this animal that he plunged into the river only a few feet behind the second man he had compelled to take refuge in the water, when one of those who remained on shore shot him through the head and finally killed him. They then took him on shore and butchered him when they found eight balls had passed through him in different directions.

Lewis, May 14, 1805

We set out at an early hour and proceeded on very well. We employed the tow line the greater part of the day. The banks were firm and the shore bald which favored the use of the cord. I find this method of ascending the river, when the shore is such as will permit it, the safest and most expeditious mode of traveling, except with sails in a steady and favorable breeze.

Lewis, May 16, 1805

May 17, 1805, mile 2209

Fort Peck Lake reaches 134 miles up the Missouri River. It took Lewis and Clark ten days to ascend the Missouri from the site of the dam to the upper end of the lake.

May 18, 1805, mile 2213

Clark almost stepped on a rattlesnake in this area, and another one was killed in camp on May 17. These were probably prairie rattlesnakes. Lewis made very detailed descriptions of the plant and animals they encountered, sometimes running 1,000 or 1,500 words in length. Many of these animals were new to the science of the day.

May 18, 1805, mile 2229

Captain Clark narrowly escaped being bitten by a rattlesnake in the course of his walk. The party killed one this evening at our encampment, which Clark informed me was similar to that he had seen. This snake is smaller than those common to the middle Atlantic states, being about 2 feet 6 inches long. It is of a yellowish brown color on the back and sides, variegated with one row of oval spots of a dark brown color lying transversely over the back from the neck to the tail, and two other rows of small, circular spots of the same color which garnish the sides along the edge of the scuta. There are 176 scuta on its belly and 17 on the tail.

Lewis, May 17, 1805

We were roused late at night by the sergeant of the guard, and warned of the danger we were in from a large tree that had taken fire and which leaned immediately over our lodge. We had the lodge removed, and a few minutes after, a large proportion of the top of a tree fell on the place the lodge had stood. Had we been a few minutes later we should have been crushed to atoms.

The wind blew so hard, that notwithstanding the lodge was fifty paces distance from the fire, it sustained considerable injury from the burning coals which were thrown on it. The party were much harassed also by this fire, which communicated to a collection of fallen timber and could not be extinguished.

Lewis, May 17, 1805

The country is rugged, the hills high, their summits and sides partially covered with pine and cedar, the river on either side washing their bases. It is somewhat singular that the lower part of these hills appear to be formed of a dark, rich loam while at the upper region about 150 feet is formed of a whitish brown sand, so hard in many parts as to resemble stone; but little rock or stone of any kind is to be seen in these hills.

Lewis, May 16, 1805

May 21, 1805, mile 2270

The Missouri gradually transforms from lake to river at the upper end of Fort Peck Lake.

I walked out after dinner and ascended a butte a few miles off to view the country, which I found rolling and of a very rich sticky soil producing but little vegetation of any kind except the prickly pear. There is but little grass, and that is very low. There is a great deal of scattering pine on the larboard side and some few on the starboard side.

Clark, May 22, 1805

The frost was severe last night. The ice appeared along the edge of the water, and water also froze on the oars. We passed the entrance of a creek 15 yards wide on the starboard side. This we called Teapot Creek. It affords no water at its mouth, but has running water at some small distance above. This I believe to be the case with many of those creeks which we have passed since we entered this hilly country. The water is absorbed by the earth near the river and, of course, appears dry. They afford but little water at any rate, and that is so strongly impregnated with these salts that it is unfit for use. All the wild animals appear fond of this water. I have tried it by way of experiment and find it moderately purgative, but painful to the intestines and their operation.

Lewis, May 23, 1805

May 23, 1805, mile 2298

May 22, 1805, mile 2281

Into the Mountains...

Western Montana

The expedition steadily ascended the Missouri to Great Falls, where they spent almost a month on an 18-mile portage around the falls and rapids. Then they continued as far as practical up the river, and finally left the last of their canoes behind on August 24, 1805 to start across the Continental Divide at Lemhi Pass.

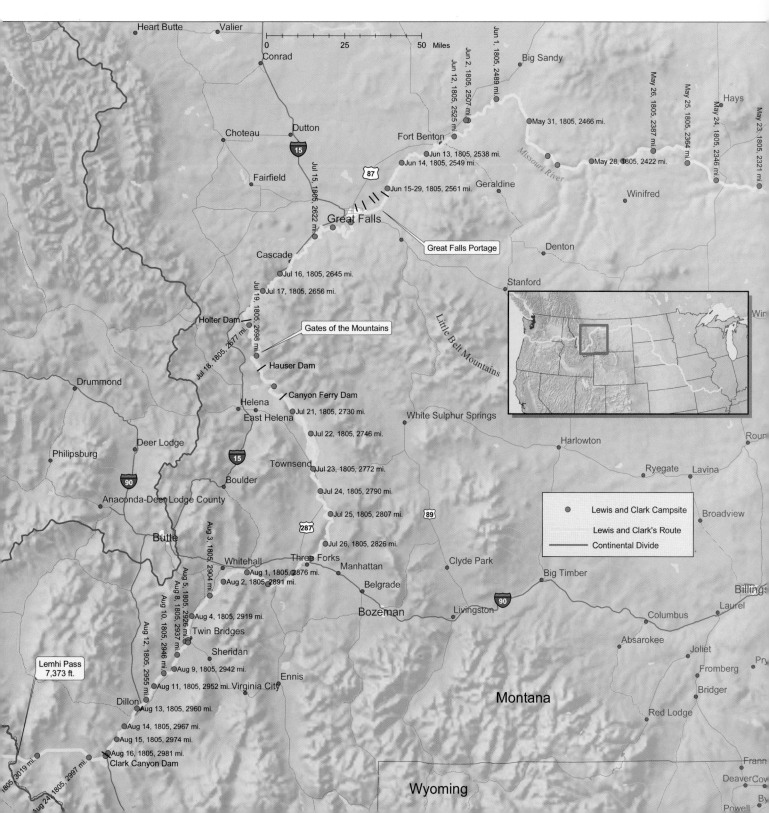

Fort Peck Lake becomes grassy wetlands at its far upper end. The creeks in this area were typically dry, or nearly so, when Lewis and Clark came through.

May 23, 1805, mile 2299

> The creek takes its rise in the mountains which are situated in a northwardly direction from its entrance, a distance of about 30 miles. The air is so pure in this open country that mountains and other elevated objects appear much nearer than they really are. These mountains do not appear to be further than 15 miles. We sent a man up this creek to explore the country. He returned late in the evening and informed that he had proceeded 10 miles directly towards these mountains and that he did not think himself by any means half way. These mountains are rocky and covered with some scattering pine. This stream we call North Mountain Creek.
>
> *Lewis, May 24, 1805*

May 23, 1805, mile 2307

Rock Creek, named North Mountain Creek by Lewis and Clark, enters the Missouri a few miles west of this bend. Antoine Butte, with an elevation of 5,743 feet, is the largest of a small group of mountains 23 miles to the north.

May 24, 1805, mile 2341

The expedition logged 24.5 miles on May 24, 1805, although their logged mile is consistently shorter than the standard mile due to their methods of measurement.

The Highway 191 Bridge is one of the few bridges across the Missouri between Fort Peck Dam and Fort Benton. The Upper Missouri River Breaks National Monument, created in 2001, includes the Missouri River from this bridge to Fort Benton, 149 miles upstream.

May 24, 1805, mile 2337

We set out at an early hour this morning and proceeded on principally by the cord until about 9 a.m. when a fine breeze sprung up from the southeast and enabled us through the balance of the day to employ our sails to advantage. We proceeded at a pretty good pace, notwithstanding the current of the river being very strong.

Game is becoming more scarce, particularly beaver, of which we have seen but few for several days. The beaver appears to keep pace with the timber. As the timber declines in quantity the beaver also become more scarce.

Lewis, May 24, 1805

May 25, 1805, mile 2348

May 25, 1805, mile 2354

The expedition camped just below Lower Two Calf Island, shown here, on May 24, 1805

As we ascended the river today I saw several gangs of the big horned animals on the face of the steep bluffs and cliffs on the starboard side, and sent Drouillard to kill one, which he accomplished. Captain Clark and Bratton, who were on shore, each killed one of these animals this evening. The head and horns of the male which Drouillard killed weighed 27 lbs.

The places they generally collect to lodge is the crannies or crevices of the rocks in the faces of inaccessible precipices, where the wolf nor bear can reach them and where indeed man himself would in many instances find a similar deficiency; yet these animals bound from rock to rock and stand apparently in the most careless manner on the sides of precipices of many hundred feet. They are very shy and are quick of both scent and sight.

Lewis, May 25, 1805

Grand Island, above, was called Big Horn Island by Lewis and Clark.

May 25, 1805, mile 2353

This abandoned homestead is in the river bottom near Grand Island.

May 25, 1805, mile 2353

May 26, 1805, mile 2370

The country on either hand is high, broken, and rocky. The rock is either soft brown sandstone covered with a thin strata of limestone, or a hard, black, rugged granite, both usually in horizontal stratas, and the sandy rock overlaying the other.

Lewis, May 25, 1805

May 26, 1805, mile 2370

This view shows the various layers of rocks and minerals, and a precarious road above the river.

In the mid to late 1800's, Cow Island, shown above, served as the head of Missouri River navigation during the low-water period in the fall. In 1877 some of the Nez Perce Indians crossed the river here on their way to Canada to escape forced relocation onto the Idaho reservations.

May 28, 1805, mile 2404

The view above is probably similar to the one Clark and Lewis saw, with the high mountains in the distant background. The odd thing about the journal entries of May 26th is that both men wrote that they climbed to a high plain, saw the same thing, and felt the same trepidation, using almost identical language. It is possible that they each climbed to see the mountains, and Clark then copied some of his journal entry from Lewis. The Mountains they reported seeing are the Little Belt Mountains on the eastern edge of the Rockies.

The river is enclosed with very high hills on either side. I took one man and walked out this morning, and ascended the high country to view the mountains which I thought I saw yesterday. From the first summit of the hill I could plainly see the mountains on either side which I saw yesterday and at no great distance from me. Those on the starboard side are an irregular range, the two extremities of which bore west and northwest from me. Those mountains on the larboard side appeared to be several detached knobs or mountains rising from a level open country, at different distances from me, from southwest to southeast. On one, the most southwesterly of those mountains, there appeared to be snow.

I crossed a deep hollow and ascended a part of the plain elevated much higher than where I first viewed the above mountains. From this point I beheld the Rocky Mountains for the first time with certainty. I could only discover a few of the most elevated points above the horizon, the most remarkable of which by my pocket compass I found bore south 60° west. Those points of the Rocky Mountains were covered with snow and the sun shown on it in such a manner as to give me a most plain and satisfactory view.

Whilst I viewed those mountains, I felt a secret pleasure in finding myself so near the head of the heretofore conceived boundless Missouri. But when I reflected on the difficulties which this snowy barrier would most probably throw in my way to the Pacific Ocean, and the sufferings and hardships of myself and the party in them, it in some measure counterbalanced the joy I had felt in the first moments in which I gazed on them. But as I have always held it little short of criminality to anticipate evils, I will allow it to be a good comfortable road until I am compelled to believe otherwise.

Clark, May 26, 1805

May 26, 1805, mile 2380

May 26, 1805, mile 2382

This country may with propriety, I think, be termed the Deserts of America, as I do not conceive any part can ever be settled. It is deficient in water and timber, and too steep to be tilled.

Clark, May 26, 1805

It was dark before we finished butchering the buffalo. On my return to camp I trod within a few inches of a rattlesnake, but being in motion I passed before he could probably put himself in a striking attitude, and fortunately escaped his bite. I struck about with my spontoon, being directed in some measure by his noise, until I killed him.

Lewis, May 26, 1805

May 26, 1805, mile 2381

May 26, 1805, mile 2381

We set out early in a fine morning and passed through a desert country, in which there is no timber on any part except a few scattered pines on the hills. We saw few animals of any kind, but the ibex or mountain sheep. One of our men killed a male which had horns two feet long and four inches in diameter at the root. At dark we came to large rapids, where we had to unite the crews of two or three canoes to force them through. It was sometime after night when we could encamp.

Gass, May 26, 1805

May 28, 1805, mile 2402

We flew from Glasgow to Bozeman on June 12. For most of the day we battled 20-30 mph headwinds. Since our cruise airspeed was 60 to 80 mph, this cut our range by about 30 percent. We carried some gasoline with us so we could land in a field or airstrip and fuel up. Otherwise we wouldn't be able to make it safely from one fuel stop to the next in this area.

We found a nice, dry field (above) and made a low pass to check for mud, rocks, holes, etc. We decided it was safe and came around to land. As soon as the wheels touched, mud started flying. The field had a dry crust on top of wet mud. We immediately took off and landed at Winifred (below), a very friendly town.

May 28, 1805, mile 2402

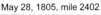

The Winifred, Montana airport is the grass strip near the center of this photo. The school is on the right side of the picture, the home of the Red Raiders. The football field is between the school and the airport.

May 28, 1805, mile 2402

Today we had difficult water and passed through the most dismal country I ever beheld; nothing but barren mountains on both sides of the river, as far as our view could extend.

Gass, May 27, 1805

The bluffs are very high, steep, and rugged, containing considerable quantities of stone and border the river closely on both sides. Once, perhaps, in the course of several miles there will be a few acres of tolerably level land in which two or three impoverished cottonwood trees will be seen. Great quantities of stone also lie in the river and garnish its borders.

Lewis, May 27, 1805

This rugged land borders the Missouri River across from the expedition's May 27 camp.

May 28, 1805, mile 2402

May 28, 1805, mile 2404

The river snakes through higher ground of the Missouri Breaks.

I walked on shore and found the country rugged and as described yesterday. I saw great numbers of the big horned animals, one of which I killed. Their fawns are nearly half grown.

Clark, May 28, 1805

Last night we were all alarmed by a large buffalo bull which swam over from the opposite shore, and coming along side of the white pirogue, climbed over it to land. He then alarmed, ran up the bank in full speed directly towards the fires, and was within 18 inches of the heads of some of the men who lay sleeping, before the sentinel could alarm him or make him change his course. Still more alarmed, he now took his direction immediately towards our lodge, passing between four fires and within a few inches of the heads of one range of the men as they yet lay sleeping. When he came near the tent, my dog saved us by causing him to change his course a second time, which he did by turning a little to the right, as quickly out of sight.

We were left by this time all in an uproar with our guns in our hands, inquiring of each other the cause of the alarm, which after a few moments was explained by the sentinel. We were happy to find no one hurt. The next morning we found that the buffalo, in passing the pirogue, had trodden on a rifle which belonged to Captain Clark's black man, who had negligently left her in the pirogue. The rifle was much bent. He had also broken the spindle, pivot, and shattered the stock of one of the blunderbusses on board. With this damage I felt well content, happy indeed, that we had sustained no further injury. It appears that the white pirogue, which contains our most valuable stores, is attended by some evil genie.

Lewis, May 29, 1805

May 27, 1805, mile 2401

The McClelland (or Stafford) Ferry, seen here in the distance, has been moving people across the Missouri since 1915. It is located north of Winifred, Montana on Highway 240.

Today we employed the cord generally, to which we also gave the assistance of the pole at the riffles and rocky points. These are numerous, and many of them are much worse than those we passed yesterday. Around those points the water drives with great force, and we are obliged in many instances to steer our vessels through the apertures formed by the points of large sharp rocks which reach a few inches above the surface of the water. Here, should our cord give way, the bow is instantly driven outwards by the stream and the vessel thrown with her side on the rocks where she must inevitably be overset or perhaps be dashed to pieces.

Our ropes are but slender, all of them except one being made of elk's skin and much worn. Frequently wet and exposed to the heat of the weather, they are weak and rotten. They have given way several times in the course of the day, but happily at such places that the vessel had room to wheel free of the rocks and therefore escaped injury. With every precaution we can take it is with much labor and infinite risk that we are enabled to get around these points.

One of our party saw a very large bear today, but being some distance from the river and no timber to conceal him, he did not think it proper to fire on him.

Lewis, May 28, 1805

May 29, 1805, mile 2432

Clark named the Judith River, a few miles downstream from here, after the 13-year-old Julia Hancock from Virginia. She later married Clark.

We passed a handsome river which discharged itself on the larboard side. I walked on shore and ascended this river about a mile and a half in order to examine it. The water of this river is clearer than any we have met with. There is a great abundance of big horned animals in the high country through which this river passes. Captain Clark, who ascended this river much higher than I did, has thought it proper to call it Judith's River.

On the Missouri, just above the entrance of the Judith River, I counted the remains of the fires of 126 Indian lodges which appeared to be of very recent date, perhaps 12 or 15 days. Captain Clark also saw a large encampment just above the entrance of this river on the starboard side of rather older date. Probably they were the same Indians.

Lewis, May 29, 1805

Today we passed on the starboard side the remains of a vast many mangled carcasses of buffalo which had been driven over a precipice of 120 feet by the Indians and perished. The water appeared to have washed away a part of this immense pile of slaughter, and still there remained the fragments of at least a hundred carcasses. They created a most horrid stench.

In this manner the Indians of the Missouri destroy vast herds of buffalo at a stroke: For this purpose, one of the most active and fleet young men is selected and disguised in a robe of buffalo skin, having also the skin of the buffalo's head with the ears and horns fastened on his head in the form of a cap. Thus caparisoned, he places himself at a convenient distance between a herd of buffalo and a precipice proper for that purpose, which happens in many places on this river for miles together. The other Indians now surround the herd on the back and flanks. At a signal agreed on, all show themselves at the same time, moving forward towards the buffalo.

The disguised Indian or decoy has taken care to place himself sufficiently nigh the buffalo to be noticed by them when they take to flight. Running before them, the buffalo follow him in full speed to the precipice. The cattle behind driving those in front over and seeing them go, do not look or hesitate about following until the whole are precipitated down the precipice, forming one common mass of dead and mangled carcasses. The decoy, in the mean time, has taken care to secure himself in some cranny or crevice of the cliff which he had previously prepared for that purpose. The part of the decoy, I am informed, is extremely dangerous. If they are not very fleet runners, the buffalo tread them under foot and crush them to death, and sometimes drive them over the precipice also, where they perish with the buffalo.

Just above this place we came to for dinner, opposite the entrance of a bold running river, 40 yards wide, which falls in on the larboard side. This stream we call the Slaughter River.

Lewis, May 29, 1805

Great numbers of wolves were about this place and very gentle. I killed one of them with my spear.

Clark, May 29, 1805

May 29, 1805, mile 2439

The Slaughter River, now called Arrow Creek, flows into the Missouri at the left of this photo. The Indians drove the herds of buffalo over the cliff on the right.

The air of the open country is astonishingly dry as well as pure. The water of the river still continues to become clearer and, notwithstanding the rain which has fallen, it is still much clearer than it was a few days past.

Lewis, May 30, 1805

May 30, 1805, mile 2442

May 30, 1805, mile 2442

Although this looks like smooth sailing, our trip through the Missouri Breaks was very turbulent with a strong northwest wind. Even so, it was infinitely easier for us than for Lewis and Clark.

The wind was too high for us to proceed until about 11 o'clock, at which time we set out and proceeded on with great labor. We were obliged to make use of the tow rope, and the banks were so muddy and slippery that the men could scarcely walk. Notwithstanding, we proceeded on as well as we could. The wind was hard from the northwest. In attempting to ascend a rapid, our tow cord broke and we turned without injury. Those rapids or shoaly points are numerous and difficult, one being at the mouth of every drain.

There was some little rain at times all day. One man ascended the high country, and it was raining and snowing on those hills. The day has proved to be raw and cold. Back from the river the land is tolerably level. There is no timber of any kind on the hills, and only a few scattering of cottonwood, willow, and ash near the river.

Clark, May 30, 1805

A canoe is dwarfed by the massive riverbank.

May 30, 1805, mile 2446

May 30, 1805, mile 2445

Rock formations of
the Missouri Breaks

May 30, 1805, mile 2445

May 30, 1805, mile 2447

No part of this Missouri from the Minetares to this place furnishes a permanent residence for any nation, yet there is no part of it but what exhibits appearances of being occasionally visited by some nation on hunting excursions.

Lewis, May 30, 1805

May 30, 1805, mile 2448

May 30, 1805, mile 2448

The obstructions of rocky points and riffles still continue as yesterday. At those places the men are compelled to be in the water even to their armpits, and the water is yet very cold. So frequent are those points that they are one fourth of their time in the water. Added to this, the banks and bluffs along which they are obliged to pass are so slippery and the mud so tenacious that they are unable to wear their moccasins. In that situation [barefoot], they are dragging the heavy burden of a canoe and walking occasionally for several hundred yards over the sharp fragments of rocks which tumble from the cliffs and garnish the borders of the river. In short, their labor is incredibly painful and great, yet those faithful fellows bear it without a murmur.

The tow rope of the white pirogue, the only one indeed of hemp, and that on which we most depended, gave way today at a bad point, the pirogue swung and but slightly touched a rock, yet was very near oversetting. I fear her evil genie will play so many pranks with her that she will go to the bottom some of those days.

Captain Clark walked on shore this morning but found it so excessively bad that he shortly returned. At 12 o'clock we came to for refreshment and gave the men a dram, which, they received with much cheerfulness and well deserved.

Lewis, May 31, 1805

The hills and river cliffs which we passed today exhibit a most romantic appearance. The bluffs of the river rise to the height of from 200 to 300 feet, and in most places nearly perpendicular. They are formed of remarkable white sandstone which is sufficiently soft to give way readily to the impression of water. Two or three thin horizontal stratas of white freestone, on which the rains or water make no impression, lie imbedded in these cliffs of soft stone near the upper part of them. The earth on the top of these Cliffs is a dark rich loam, which forming a gradually ascending plain extends back from half a mile to a mile, where the hills commence and rise abruptly to a height of about 300 feet more.

Lewis, May 31, 1805

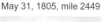
May 31, 1805, mile 2449

The water, in the course of time in descending from those hills and plains on either side of the river, has trickled down the soft sand cliffs and worn it into a thousand grotesque figures, which with the help of a little imagination and an oblique view, at a distance are made to represent elegant ranges of lofty freestone buildings, having their parapets well stocked with statuary. Columns of various sculpture, both grooved and plain, are also seen supporting long galleries in front of those buildings

Lewis, May 31, 1805
(continued...)

May 31, 1805, mile 2450

In other places on a much nearer approach and with the help of less imagination, we see the remains or ruins of elegant buildings. There are some columns standing and almost entire with their pedestals and capitals, others retaining their pedestals but deprived by time or accident of their capitals, some lying prostrate and broken, and others in the form of vast pyramids of conic structure bearing a series of other pyramids on their tops, becoming less as they ascend and finally terminating in a sharp point.

Lewis, May 31, 1805 (continued...)

May 31, 1805, mile 2449

Niches and alcoves of various forms and sizes are seen at different heights as we pass. A number of the small martins which build their nests with clay in a globular form attached to the wall within those niches, and which were seen hovering about the tops of the columns, did not the less remind us of some of those large stone buildings in the United States.

Lewis, May 31, 1805
(continued...)

The thin stratas of hard freestone intermixed with the soft sandstone seems to have aided the water in forming this curious scenery. As we passed on, it seemed as if those scenes of visionary enchantment would never have an end, for here it is too that nature presents to the view of the traveler vast ranges of walls of tolerable workmanship. So perfect indeed are those walls that I should have thought that nature had attempted here to rival the human art of masonry had I not recollected that she had first begun her work. These walls rise to the height in many places of 100 feet, are perpendicular, with two regular faces and are from 1 to 12 feet thick. Each wall retains the same thickness at top which it possesses at bottom.

Lewis, May 31, 1805 (continued...)

May 31, 1805, mile 2462

The stone of which these walls are formed is black, dense, and durable, and appears to be composed of a large portion of earth intermixed or cemented with a small quantity of sand and a considerable portion of talc or quartz. These stones are almost invariably regular parallelepipeds, of unequal sizes in the walls but equal in their horizontal ranges, at least as to depth. These are laid regularly in ranges on each other like bricks, each breaking or covering the interstice of the two on which it rests, thus the perpendicular interstices are broken, and the horizontal ones extend entire throughout the whole extent of the walls. These stones seem to bear some proportion to the thickness of the walls in which they are employed, being larger in the thicker walls. The greatest length of the parallelepiped appears to form the thickness of the thinner walls, while two or more are employed to form that of the thicker walls.

These walls pass the river in several places, rising from the water's edge much above the sandstone bluffs, which they seem to penetrate; thence continuing their course on a straight line on either side of the river through the gradually ascending plains, over which they tower to the height of from ten to seventy feet until they reach the hills, which they finally enter and conceal themselves. These walls sometimes run parallel to each other, with several ranges near each other, and at other times intersecting each other at right angles, having the appearance of the walls of ancient houses or gardens.

Lewis, May 31, 1805

May 31, 1805, mile 2466

I walked on shore this evening and examined these walls minutely and preserved a specimen of the stone. I found the face of many of the river hills formed of cliffs of very excellent free stone of a light yellowish brown color. On these cliffs I met with a species of pine which I had never seen. It differs from the pitch pine in the particular of its leaf and cone, the first being vastly shorter, and the latter considerably longer and more pointed.

I saw near those bluffs the most beautiful fox that I ever beheld. The colors appeared to me to be a fine orange yellow, white and black. I endeavored to kill this animal but it discovered me at a considerable distance. Finding that I could get no nearer, I fired on him as he ran and missed him. He concealed himself under the rocks of the cliff. It appeared to me to be about the size of the common red fox of the Atlantic states, or rather smaller than the large fox common to this country, convinced I am that it is a distinct species.

Lewis, May 31, 1805

These formations and those at the top of the page are across from the expedition's campsite of May 31, 1805.

May 31, 1805, mile 2465

June 1, 1805, mile 2468

June 1, 1805, mile 2470

We set out at an early hour and proceeded on as usual with the tow rope. The country appears to be lower and the cliffs not so high or common.

Clark, June 1, 1805

June 1, 1805, mile 2470

June 1, 1805, mile 2475

A thunderstorm builds on Baldy Mountain, the mountain Clark described on June 1, 1805. It is the highest peak of the Bearpaw Mountains near Big Sandy, Montana.

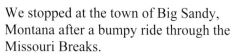

A mountain or a part of the north mountains is about 8 or 10 miles north of this place.

Clark, June 1, 1805

June 1, 1805, mile 2475

We stopped at the town of Big Sandy, Montana after a bumpy ride through the Missouri Breaks.

We employed the cord, as usual, the greater part of the day. The current was strong, though regular, and the banks afforded us good towing. The river bluffs still continue to get lower and the plains leveler and more extensive. The timber on the river increases in quantity.

Lewis, June 2, 1805

The bear was very near catching Drouillard. It also pursued Charbonneau, who fired his gun in the air as he ran. He fortunately eluded the vigilance of the bear by secreting himself very securely in the bushes until Drouillard finally killed it by a shot in the head, the only shot indeed that will conquer the ferocity of those tremendous animals.

Lewis, June 2, 1805

By this time, grizzly bears had earned a great deal of respect from the expedition. When they were first told of the grizzlies by the Indians, the men of the expedition assumed their superior weapons would be no match for the bears. Now they avoided confrontations as often as not.

June 2, 1805, mile 2503

Lewis and Clark got to this point, where the Marias and Teton rivers enter the Missouri, and were not sure which way to go. It could have been very costly to make the wrong turn. When they passed the Milk River hundreds of miles back, they assumed it was the one the Indians called "the river that scolds all others." In fact, the Indians were talking about the Marias River here.

June 2, 1805, mile 2507

This morning early we passed over and formed a camp on the point formed by the junction of the two large rivers. An interesting question was now to be determined: which of these rivers was the Missouri, the river the Minetares call a *mahte arz-zha*, that they had described to us as approaching very near to the Columbia River?

To mistake the stream at this period of the season, two months of the traveling season having now elapsed, and to ascend such stream to the Rocky Mountains or perhaps much farther before we could inform ourselves whether it did approach the Columbia or not, and then be obliged to return and take the other stream would not only lose us the whole of this season, but would probably so dishearten the party that it might defeat the expedition altogether.

Lewis, June 3, 1805

The expedition, or parts of it, spent eight nights here. Both Lewis and Clark believed the left fork in the river to be the Missouri, which was correct. The other members of the expedition, with the possible exception of Lewis's dog, believed the right fork to be the proper path. Lewis and Clark decided to scout out both the rivers on foot and look for the "great falls" described to them by the Indians. Walking was much faster than taking the boats up the rivers.

Clark took five men up the Missouri, and Lewis took six men about 60 miles up the Marias River. Clark got within 10 miles of the first falls without seeing them, but he was nevertheless convinced it was the Missouri.

A view up the mouth of the Marias River.   June 2, 1805, mile 2507

Goodrich has caught a considerable quantity of small fish. Some of them are scale fish, but the most part are a sort of smallish sized catfish. We have caught no large ones this season as we did last, as yet.

Whitehouse, June 5, 1805

I now became well convinced that this branch of the Missouri had its direction too much to the north for our route to the Pacific, and therefore determined to return the next day after taking an observation of the sun's meridian altitude in order to fix the latitude of the place.

Lewis, June 6, 1805

On his exploration north, Lewis thought it was important to get an accurate position, particularly latitude, of his northernmost exploration because the Louisiana Purchase included all the land drained by the Missouri. President Thomas Jefferson was hoping to define the border between U.S. territory and Canada as far north as possible, so he asked Lewis to find the northernmost point of the Missouri drainage. On his return trip from the Pacific, Lewis took a group and explored farther north up the Marias River. On that trip they beat a hasty retreat down the river after a deadly encounter with the Blackfeet Indians.

We left our watery beds at an early hour and continued our route down the river. It still continues to rain, the wind hard from the northeast and cold. The ground is remarkable slippery, insomuch that we were unable to walk on the sides of the bluffs where we had passed as we ascended the river. Notwithstanding the rain that has now fallen, the earth of these bluffs is not wet to a greater depth than two inches. In its present state it is precisely like walking over frozen ground which is thawed to a small depth and slips equally as bad. This clay not only appears to require more water to saturate it than any earth I ever observed, but when saturated it appears on the other hand to yield its moisture with equal difficulty.

In passing along the face of one of these bluffs today, I slipped at a narrow pass of about 30 yards in length, and but for a quick and fortunate recovery by means of my spontoon, I should have been precipitated into the river down a craggy precipice of about 90 feet. I had scarcely reached a place where I could stand with tolerable safety, even with the assistance of my spontoon, before I heard a voice behind me cry out, "God, God Captain, what shall I do?" On turning about I found it was Windsor who had slipped and fallen about the center of this narrow pass. He was lying prostrate on his belly, with his right hand, arm, and leg over the precipice while he was holding on with the left arm and foot as well as he could, which appeared to be with much difficulty.

I discovered his danger, and the trepidation which he was in gave me still further concern, for I expected every instant to see him lose his strength and slip off. Although much alarmed at his situation, I disguised my feelings and spoke very calmly to him, that he was in no kind of danger, to take the knife out of his belt behind him with his right hand and dig a hole with it in the face of the bank to receive his right foot, which he did and then raised himself to his knees. I then directed him to take off his moccasins and to come forward on his hand and knees, holding the knife in one hand and the gun with the other. This he happily effected and escaped. Those who were some little distance behind returned by my orders and waded the river at the foot of the bluff, where the water was breast deep.

Lewis coming down the Marias River, June 7, 1805

The whole of my party to a man except myself were fully persuaded that this river was the Missouri, but being fully of opinion that it was neither the main stream nor that which would be advisable for us to take, I determined to give it a name and in honor of Miss Maria Wood, called it Maria's River.

Lewis, June 8, 1805

We determined to deposit at this place the large red pirogue, all the heavy baggage we could possibly do without, and some provisions, salt, tools, powder, lead, etc.; with a view to lighten our vessels, and at the same time to strengthen their crews by means of the seven hands who have been heretofore employed in navigating the red pirogue. Accordingly, we set some hands to digging a hole or cellar for the reception of our stores.

Lewis, June 9, 1805

Those ideas [reasons to take the south fork], as they occurred to me, I endeavored to impress on the minds of the party, all of whom except Captain Clark being still firm in the belief that the north fork was the Missouri and that which we ought to take. They said very cheerfully that they were ready to follow us anywhere we thought proper to direct, but that they still thought that the other was the river and that they were afraid that the south fork would soon terminate in the mountains and leave us a great distance from the Columbia.

Finding them so determined in this belief, and wishing that if we were in error to be able to detect it and rectify it as soon as possible, it was agreed between Captain Clark and myself that one of us should set out with a small party by land up the south fork and continue our route up it until we found the falls or reached the snowy mountains, by which means we should be enabled to determine this question pretty accurately. This expedition I preferred undertaking as Captain Clark is the best waterman.

Lewis, June 9, 1805

We encamped in an old Indian lodge made of sticks and bark. At the river near our camp we saw two white bear [grizzlies]. One of them was nearly catching Joseph Fields. Joseph Fields could not fire, as his gun was wet. The bear was so near that it struck his foot. We were not in a situation to give him assistance, a cliff of rocks separating us. The bear got alarmed at our shot and yells, and took to the river.

There was some little rain and snow last night. The mountains to our southeast are covered with snow this morning. It is very cold and raining a little. We saw 8 buffalo on the opposite side of the river. They made two attempts to cross, the water being so swift they could not. About the time we were setting out, *three* white bears approached our camp. We killed the three, ate part of one, and set out.

Clark, June 4, 1805

June 13, 1805, mile 2530

On Clark's scouting mission, he went up the Missouri past what is now Fort Benton. On June 4 they were camped about 10 miles south (upriver) of Fort Benton when Joseph Fields narrowly escaped an angry (or hungry) bear. The next day they got within 10 miles of the first falls when they turned around, convinced that this was truly the Missouri River.

June 14, 1805, mile 2543

We saw an immense number of swallows in the first bluff on the larboard side. The water is very swift. The bluffs are blackish clay and coal for about 80 feet. The earth above that for about 30 or 40 feet is a brownish yellow. There are a number of bars of coarse gravel and stones of different shapes and sizes. We saw a number of rattlesnakes today. One of the men caught one by the head, by catching hold of a bush on which his head lay reclined. Three canoes were in great danger today. One dipped water and another was very near turning over. The interpreter's woman (Sacagawea) is very sick, worse than she has been.

Clark, June 12, 1805

June 13, 1805, mile 2532

The bluffs are just as Clark described. They extend intermittently for several miles on either side of Fort Benton, Montana.

June 13, 1805, mile 2531

On this plain there were "infinitely more buffalo" than Lewis had ever seen. Morony Dam can be seen on the river in the distance. Portage Creek, now called Belt Creek, branches off to the left of the river about half way to Morony Dam. Lewis and Clark began their 18-mile portage in this area.

June 15, 1805, mile 2561

June 30, 1805, mile 2563

We can hear the falls this morning very distinctly. The current is excessively rapid and difficult to ascend. There are great numbers of dangerous places, and the fatigue which we have to encounter is incredible. The men are in the water from morning until night, hauling the cord and boats, walking on sharp rocks and round slippery stones which alternately cut their feet and throw them down. Notwithstanding all this difficulty, they go with great cheerfulness. Added to those difficulties, the rattlesnakes are innumerable and require great caution to prevent being bitten.

The Indian woman is much worse this evening. She will not take any medicine. Her husband petitions to return.

Clark, June 15, 1805

Morony Dam, constructed in 1930, is the northernmost, or farthest downstream, of the five dams in the Great Falls area.

June 30, 1805, mile 2567

This canyon leads up to the Great Falls, now capped by Ryan Dam.

Lewis's Discovery of the Great Falls of the Missouri

This morning we set out about sunrise after taking breakfast off our venison and fish. We again ascended the hills of the river and gained the level country, the country through which we passed for the first 6 miles. Though more rolling than that we had passed yesterday, it might still with propriety be deemed a level country. Our course, as yesterday, was generally southwest. The river from the place we left it appeared to make a considerable bend to the south.

From the extremity of this rolling country I overlooked a most beautiful and level plain of great extent, at least 50 or 60 miles. In this there were infinitely more buffalo than I had ever before witnessed at a view. Nearly in the direction I had been traveling or southwest two curious mountains presented themselves of square figures, the sides rising perpendicularly to the height of 250 feet and appeared to be formed of yellow clay. Their tops appeared to be level plains. These inaccessible heights appeared like the ramparts of immense fortifications. I have no doubt but with very little assistance from art they might be rendered impregnable.

Fearing that the river bore to the south and that I might pass the falls if they existed between this and the snowy mountains, I altered my course nearly to the south, leaving those insulated hills to my right and proceeded through the plain. I sent Fields on my right and Drouillard and Gibson on my left with orders to kill some meat and join me at the river, where I should halt for dinner. I had proceeded on this course about 2 miles, with Goodrich at some distance behind me, when my ears were saluted with the agreeable sound of a fall of water. Advancing a little further I saw the spray arise above the plain like a column of smoke. It would frequently disappear again in an instant, caused, I presume, by the wind which blew pretty hard from the southwest.

I did not, however, lose my direction to this point, which soon began to make a roaring too tremendous to be mistaken for any cause short of the Great Falls of the Missouri. Here I arrived about 12 o'clock having traveled by estimate about 15 miles. I hurried down the hill, which was about 200 feet high and difficult of access, to gaze on this sublimely grand spectacle. I took my position on the top of some rocks about 20 feet high, opposite the center of the falls.

This chain of rocks appears once to have formed a part of those over which the waters tumbled, but in the course of time has been separated from it to the distance of 150 yards, lying parallel to it and an abutment against which the water after falling over the precipice beats with great fury. This barrier extends on the right to the perpendicular cliff which forms that border of the river, but to the distance of 120 yards next to the cliff it is but a few feet above the level of the water.

Here the water in very high tides appears to pass in a channel of 40 yards next to the higher part of the ledge of rocks. On the left extends within 80 or 90 yards of the larboard a cliff, which is also perpendicular. Between this abrupt extremity of the ledge of rocks and the perpendicular bluff the whole body of water passes with incredible swiftness. Immediately at the cascade the river is about 300 yards wide for about 90 or 100 yards. The larboard bluff is a smooth, even sheet of water falling over a precipice of at least eighty feet.

The remaining part of about 200 yards on my right forms the grandest sight I ever beheld. The height of the fall is the same as the other, but the irregular and somewhat projecting rocks below receive the water in its passage down and breaks it into a perfect white foam which assumes a thousand forms in a moment, sometimes flying up in jets of sparkling foam to the height of fifteen or twenty feet, and are scarcely formed before large rolling bodies of the same beaten and foaming water is thrown over and conceals them.

In short, the rocks seem to be most happily fixed to present a sheet of the whitest beaten froth for 200 yards in length and about 80 feet perpendicular. The water after descending strikes against the abutment before mentioned, or that on which I stand, and seems to reverberate. Being met by the more impetuous current, they roll and swell into half formed billows of great height which rise and again disappear in an instant.

This abutment of rock defends a handsome little bottom of about three acres which is diversified and agreeably shaded with some cottonwood trees. In the lower extremity of the bottom there is a very thick grove of the same kind of trees which are small. In this wood there are several Indian lodges formed of sticks, a few small cedars grow near the ledge of rocks where I rest. Below the point of these rocks at a small distance the river is divided by a large rock which rises several feet above the water, and extends downwards with the stream for about 20 yards. About a mile before the water arrives at the pitch it descends very rapidly, and is confined on the larboard side by a perpendicular cliff of about 100 feet. On the starboard side it is also perpendicular for about three hundred yards above the pitch where it is then broken by the discharge of a small ravine, down which the buffalo have a large beaten road to the water, for it is but in very few places that these animals can obtain water near this place owing to the steep and inaccessible banks.

I see several skeletons of the buffalo lying in the edge of the water near the starboard bluff, which I presume have been swept down by the current and precipitated over this tremendous fall. About 300 yards below me there is another abutment of solid rock with a perpendicular face and about 60 feet high, which projects from the starboard side at right angles to the distance of 134 yards, and terminates the lower part nearly of the bottom before mentioned. There is a passage around the end of this abutment between it and the river of about 20 yards. Here the river again assumes its usual width, soon spreading to near 300 yards, but still continues its rapidity.

From the reflection of the sun on the spray or mist which arises from these falls there is a beautiful rainbow produced, which adds not a little to the beauty of this majestically grand scenery. After writing this imperfect description I again viewed the falls and was so much disgusted with the imperfect idea which it conveyed of the scene that I determined to draw my pen across it and begin again, but then reflected that I could not perhaps succeed better than penning the first impressions of the mind. I wished for the pencil of

The Great Falls are the largest of the 5 falls in the Great Falls area, with a 96-foot vertical drop. These falls were those that Lewis first discovered, with a "roaring too tremendous to be mistaken for any cause short of the Great Falls of the Missouri." Lewis estimated their height at 80 feet. There were five waterfalls and many cascades in the Great Falls stretch of the Missouri. There are now five dams along that part of the river, including Ryan Dam pictured here.

June 30, 1805, mile 256

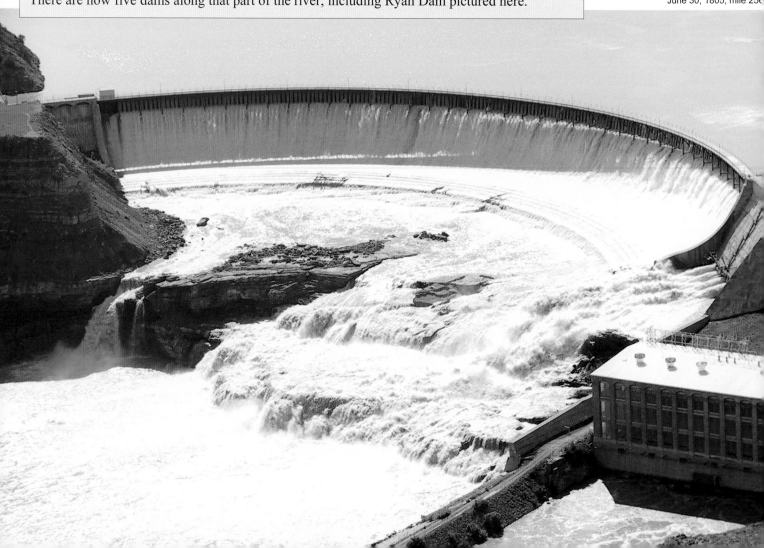

Salvador Rosa or the pen of Thompson that I might be enabled to give to the enlightened world some just idea of this truly magnificent and sublimely grand object, which has from the commencement of time been concealed from the view of civilized man, but this was fruitless and vain.

I most sincerely regretted that I had not brought a camera obscura with me, by the assistance of which even I could have hoped to have done better, but alas this was also out of my reach. I therefore, with the assistance of my pen, only endeavored to trace some of the stronger features of this scene, by the assistance of which, and my recollection aided by some able pencil, I hope still to give to the world some faint idea of an object which at this moment fills me with such pleasure and astonishment; and which of its kind I will venture to assert is second to but one in the known world.

I retired to the shade of a tree where I determined to fix my camp for the present and dispatch a man in the morning to inform Captain Clark and the party of my success in finding the falls and settle in their minds all further doubts as to the Missouri. The hunters now arrived loaded with excellent buffalo meat and informed me that they had killed three very fat cows about of a mile from hence. I directed them after they had refreshed themselves to go back and butcher them and bring another load of meat each to our camp, determining to employ those who remained with me in drying meat for the party against their arrival. In about 2 hours, or at 4 o'clock p.m., they set out on this duty.

I walked down the river about 3 miles to discover, if possible, some place to which the canoes might arrive, or at which they might be drawn on shore, in order to be taken by land above the falls; but returned without effecting either of these objects. The river was one continued scene of rapids and cascades which I readily perceived could not be encountered with our canoes, and the cliffs still retained their perpendicular structure and were from 150 to 200 feet high. In short, the river appears here to have worn a channel in the process of time through a solid rock.

On my return I found the party at camp. They had butchered the buffalo and brought in some more meat as I had directed. Goodrich had caught half a dozen very fine trout and a

number of both species of the white fish. These trout (caught in the falls) are from sixteen to twenty-three inches in length, precisely resemble our mountain or speckled trout in form and the position of their fins, but the specks on these are of a deep black instead of the red or gold color of those common to the United States. These are furnished long sharp teeth on the pallet and tongue and have generally a small dash of red on each side behind the front ventral fins. The flesh is of a pale yellowish red, or when in good order, of a rose red.

I am induced to believe that the brown, the white, and the grizzly bear of this country are the same species only differing in color from age, or more probably from the same natural cause that many other animals of the same family differ in color. One of those which we killed yesterday was of a cream colored white while the other in company with it was of the common bay or reddish brown, which seems to be the most usual color of them. The white one appeared from its talons and teeth to be the youngest. It was smaller than the other, and although a monstrous beast, we supposed that it had not yet attained its growth, and that it was a little upwards of two years old. The young cubs which we have killed have always been of a brownish white, but none of them as white as that we killed yesterday. One other that we killed sometime since, which I mentioned sunk under some driftwood and was lost, had a white stripe or list of about eleven inches wide entirely around his body just behind the shoulders, and was much darker than these bear usually are. The grizzly bear we have never yet seen. I have seen their talons in possession of the Indians and from their form I am persuaded if there is any difference between this species and the brown or white bear it is very inconsiderable. There is no such animal as a black bear in this open country or of that species generally denominated the black bear.

My fare is really sumptuous this evening: buffalo's humps, tongues, and marrowbones, fine trout, parched meal, pepper and salt, and a good appetite. The last is not considered the least of the luxuries.

Lewis, June 13, 1805

June 30, 1805, mile 2568

We saw one bear and innumerable numbers of buffalo. I saw two herds of those animals watering immediately above a considerable rapid. They descended by a narrow pass. The bottom was small and the river forced those forward into the water, some of which were taken down in an instant and seen no more. Others made shore with difficulty. I beheld 40 or 50 of those swimming at the same time. Those animals in this way are lost, and that accounts for the number of buffalo carcasses below the rapids.

Clark, June 17, 1805

Ryan Dam was built atop the Great Falls in 1915. It was originally named Volta Dam, after the 19th century physicist Alessandro Volta. In 1940 it was renamed after John D. Ryan, president of Anaconda Copper Mining from 1909 to 1933. In 1912, Ryan bought and consolidated many small hydroelectric power companies and formed the Montana Power Company. In 1928 Ryan sold his stock in Montana Power for about $85 million. In 1933, he died nearly broke, and was buried in a copper coffin. Montana Power continued to operate these dams until 2002, when Montana Power and its dams were sold to Northwestern Corporation.

This morning at sunrise I dispatched Joseph Fields with a letter to Captain Clark and ordered him to keep sufficiently near the river to observe its situation, in order that he might be enabled to give Captain Clark an idea of the point at which it would be best to halt to make our portage.

I set one man about preparing a scaffold and collecting wood to dry the meat. I sent the others to bring in the balance of the buffalo meat, or at least the part which the wolves had left us, for those fellows are ever at hand and ready to partake with us the moment we kill a buffalo. There is no means of putting the meat out of their reach in those plains. The two men shortly after returned with the meat and informed me that the wolves had devoured the greater part of the meat.

Lewis, June 14, 1805

Lewis's Exploration of the Great Falls

About ten o'clock this morning, while the men were engaged with the meat, I took my gun and spontoon and thought I would walk a few miles and see where the rapids terminated above, and return to dinner. Accordingly I set out and proceeded up the river about southwest after passing one continued rapid and three small cascades of about four or five feet each. At the distance of about 5 miles I arrived at a fall of about 19 feet. The river is here about 400 yards wide. This pitch, which I called the crooked falls, occupies about ¾ of the width of the river, commencing on the south side, extends obliquely upwards about 150 yards, then, forming an acute angle, extends downwards nearly to the commencement of four small Islands lying near the north shore.

Among these Islands, and between them and the lower extremity of the perpendicular pitch, being a distance of 100 yards or upwards, the water glides down the side of a sloping rock with a velocity almost equal to that of its perpendicular descent. Just above this rapid the river makes a sudden bend to the right or northwardly.

June 30, 1805, mile 2570

Cochrane Dam was built in 1958 across the cascades 2 miles upstream from the Great Falls. It is very similar to Morony Dam, a few miles downstream.

June 30, 1805, mile 2570

I should have returned from hence, but hearing a tremendous roaring above me, I continued my route across the point of a hill a few hundred yards further and was again presented by one of the most beautiful objects in nature, a cascade of about fifty feet perpendicular, stretching at right angles across the river from side to side, to the distance of at least a quarter of a mile. Here the river pitches over a shelving rock, with an edge as regular and as straight as if formed by art, without a niche or brake in it. The water descends in one even and uninterrupted sheet to the bottom, where dashing against the rocky bottom it rises into foaming billows of great height and rapidly glides away, hissing, flashing and sparkling. As it departs, the spray rises from one extremity to the other, to 50 feet.

I now thought that if a skillful painter had been asked to make a beautiful cascade that he would most probably have presented the precise image of this one. Nor could I for some time determine on which of those two great cataracts to bestow the palm, on this or that which I had discovered yesterday. At length I determined between these two great rivals for glory that this was pleasingly beautifully while the other was sublimely grand. I had scarcely infixed my eyes from this pleasing object before I discovered another fall above at the distance of half a mile. Thus invited I did not once think of returning but hurried thither to amuse myself with this newly discovered object.

I found this to be a cascade of about 14 feet, possessing a perpendicular pitch of about 6 feet. This was tolerably regular stretching across the river from bank to bank where it was about a quarter of a mile wide. In any other neighborhood but this, such a cascade would probably be extolled for its beauty and magnificence, but here I passed it by with but little attention, determining as I had proceeded so far, to continue my route to the head of the rapids, if it should even detain me all night.

At every rapid, cataract, and cascade, I discovered that the bluffs grew lower or that the bed of the river rose nearer to a level with the plains. Still pursuing the river with its course about southwest, passing a continued scene of rapids and small cascades, at the distance of 2½ miles I arrived at another cataract of 26 feet. This is not immediately perpendicular. A rock at about 1/3 of its decent seems to protrude to a small distance and receives the water in its passage downwards and gives a curve to the water, though it falls mostly with a regular and smooth sheet. The river is near six hundred yards wide at this place. A beautiful level plain is on the south side only a few feet above the level of the pitch. On the north side where I am, the country is more broken, and immediately behind me near the river is a high hill.

Below this fall, at a little distance, a beautiful little Island well timbered is situated about the middle of the river. In this Island on a cottonwood tree an eagle has placed her nest. A more inaccessible spot I believe she could not have found, for neither man nor beast dare pass those gulfs which separate her little domain from the shores. The water is also broken in such manner as it descends over this pitch that the mist or spray rises to a considerable height. This fall is certainly much the greatest I ever beheld except those two which I have mentioned below. It is incomparably a greater cataract and a more

noble interesting object than the celebrated falls of Potomac or Schuylkill.

Just above this is another cascade of about 5 feet, above which the water as far as I could see began to abate of its velocity. I therefore determined to

June 30, 1805, mile 2572

Crooked Falls, 26 feet high, are a few hundred yards downstream from Rainbow Dam.

ascend the hill behind me, which promised a fine prospect of the adjacent country, nor was I disappointed on my arrival at its summit. From hence I overlooked a most beautiful and extensive plain reaching from the river to the base of the snowclad mountains to the south and southwest. I also observed the Missouri stretching its meandering course to the south through this plain to a great distance, filled to its even and grassy brim.

Another large river flowed in on its western side, about 4 miles above me, and extended itself through a level and fertile valley of 3 miles in width, a great distance to the northwest, rendered more conspicuous by the timber which garnished its borders. In these plains and more particularly in the valley just below me immense herds of buffalo are feeding. The Missouri just above this hill makes a bend to the south where it lies a smooth, even, and unruffled sheet of water of nearly a mile in width, bearing on its watery bosom vast flocks of geese which feed at pleasure in the delightful pasture on either border. The young geese are now completely feathered except the wings, which both in the young and old are yet deficient.

After feasting my eyes on this ravishing prospect and resting myself a few minutes, I determined to proceed as far as the river which I saw discharge itself on the west side of the Missouri, convinced that it was the river which the Indians call Medicine River and which they informed us fell into the Missouri just above the falls. I descended the hill and directed my course to the bend of the Missouri near which there was a herd of at least a thousand buffalo. Here I thought it would be well to kill a buffalo and leave him until my return from the river, and if I then found that I had not time to get back to camp this evening, to remain all night here,

June 30, 1805, mile 2573

there being a few sticks of drift wood lying along shore which would answer for my fire, and a few scattering cottonwood trees a few hundred yards below which would afford me at least the semblance of a shelter.

This bridge was built by the Great Northern Railroad in 1902. Rainbow Dam, to the left of the bridge, was completed eight years later. Rainbow Dam provided power to copper mines more than 150 miles away, near Butte. Long-distance electrical transmission was new, and these power lines were said to be the longest in the country.

Under this impression, I selected a fat buffalo and shot him very well, through the lungs. While I was gazing attentively on the poor animal discharging blood in streams from his mouth

and nostrils, expecting him to fall every instant, and having entirely forgotten to reload my rifle, a large white, or rather, brown bear had perceived and crept on me within 20 steps before I discovered him. In the first moment I drew up my gun to shoot, but at the same instant recollected that she was not loaded and that he was too near for me to hope to perform this operation before he reached me, as he was then briskly advancing on me. It was an open level plain, not a bush within miles nor a tree within less than three hundred yards of me. The river bank was sloping and not more than three feet above the level of the water. In short, there was no place by means of which I could conceal myself from this monster until I could charge my rifle. In this situation, I thought of retreating in a brisk walk as fast as he was advancing until I could reach a tree about 300 yards below me, but I had no sooner turned myself about but he pitched at me, open mouthed and full speed.

I ran about 80 yards and found he gained on me fast. I then ran into the water. The idea struck me to get into the water to such depth that I could stand and he would be obliged to swim, and that I could in that situation defend myself with my spontoon. Accordingly, I ran hastily into the water about waist deep, and faced about and presented the point of my spontoon. At this instant he arrived at the edge of the water within about 20 feet of me. The moment I put myself in this attitude of defense he suddenly wheeled about as if frightened, declined the combat on such unequal grounds, and retreated with quite as great precipitation as he had just before pursued me. As soon as I saw him run off in that manner I returned to the shore and charged my gun, which I had still retained in my hand throughout this curious adventure. I saw him run through the level open plain about 3 miles, till he disappeared in the woods on Medicine River. During the whole of this distance he ran at full speed, sometimes appearing to look behind him as if he expected pursuit.

I now began to reflect on this novel occurrence and endeavored to account for this sudden retreat of the bear. I at first thought that perhaps he had not smelt me before he arrived at the waters edge so near me, but I then reflected that he had pursued me for about 80 or 90 yards before I took to the water, and on examination saw the ground torn with his talons immediately on the impression of my steps. The cause of his alarm still remains with me mysterious and unaccountable. So it was, and I felt myself not a little gratified that he had declined the combat. My gun reloaded, I felt confidence once more in my strength, and determined not to be thwarted in my design of visiting Medicine River, but determined never again to suffer my piece to be longer empty than the time she necessarily required to charge her. I passed through the plain nearly in the direction which the bear had run to Medicine River found it a handsome stream, about 200 yards wide with a gentle current, apparently deep, its waters clear, and banks which were formed principally of dark brown and blue clay were about the height of those of the

June 30, 1805, mile 2576

Missouri or from 3 to 5 feet. Yet they had not the appearance of ever being overflown, a circumstance, which I did not expect so immediately in the neighborhood of the mountains, from whence I should have supposed that sudden and immense torrents would issue at certain seasons of the year, but the reverse is absolutely the case. I am therefore compelled to believe that the snowy mountains yield their waters slowly, being partially effected every day by the influence of the sun only, and never suddenly melted down by hasty showers of rain.

Having examined Medicine River, I now determined to return, having by my estimate about 12 miles to walk. I looked at my watch

and found it was half after six p.m. In returning through the level bottom of Medicine River and about 200 yards distant from the Missouri, my direction led me directly to an animal that I at first supposed was a wolf, but on nearer approach or about sixty paces distant I discovered that it was not, its color was a brownish yellow. It was standing near its burrow, and when I approached it thus nearly, it couched itself down like a cat looking immediately at me as if it designed to spring on me. I took aim at it and fired, it instantly disappeared in its burrow. I loaded my gun

Black Eagle Dam is the oldest of the five "Great Falls" dams, built in 1891. The Missouri River falls more than 500 feet between here and the other side of Morony Dam, about 10 miles away.

and examined the place, which was dusty, and saw the track from which I am still further convinced that it was of the tiger kind. Whether I struck it or not I could not determine, but I am almost confident that I did. My gun is true and I had a steady rest by means of my spontoon, which I have found very serviceable to me in this way in the open plains.

It now seemed to me that all the beasts of the neighborhood had made a league to destroy me, or that some fortune was disposed to amuse herself at my expense, for I had not proceeded more than three hundred yards from the burrow of this tiger cat before three bull buffalo, which were feeding with a large herd about half a mile from me on my left, separated from the herd and ran full speed towards me. I thought at least to give them some amusement and altered my direction to meet them. When they arrived within a hundred yards they made a halt, took a good view of me, and retreated with precipitation. I then continued my route homewards passed the buffalo which I had killed, but did not think it prudent to remain all night at this place which really, from the succession of curious adventures, wore the impression on my mind of enchantment. At sometimes for a moment I thought it might be a dream, but the prickly pears which pierced my feet very severely once in a while, particularly after it grew dark, convinced me that I was really awake and that it was necessary to make the best of my way to camp.

It was sometime after dark before I returned to the party. I found them extremely uneasy for my safety. They had formed a thousand conjectures, all of which equally foreboding my death, which they had so far settled among them that they had already agreed on the route which each should take in the morning to search for me. I felt myself much fatigued, but ate a hearty supper and took a good night's rest. The weather being warm I had left my leather over shirt and had worn only a yellow flannel one.

Lewis, June 14, 1805

Great Falls, Montana surrounds Black Eagle Falls and Black Eagle Dam

June 30, 1805, mile 2576

June 30, 1805, mile 2572

Crooked Falls are in the foreground of this view, with the 48-foot Rainbow Falls and Rainbow Dam above. These are the ones Clark described on June 18.

We set out early and arrived at the second great cataract at about 200 yards above the last of 19 feet pitch. This is one of the grandest views in nature, and by far exceeds anything I ever saw: the Missouri, falling over a shelving rock for 47 feet 8 inches with a cascade of 14 feet 7 inches above the shoot for ¼ mile. I descended a cliff below this cataract with ease, measured the height of the perpendicular fall of 48 feet 8 inches at which place the river is 473 yards wide. There is a continual mist quite across this fall.

Clark, June 18, 1805

After this we proceeded on up the river a little more than a mile to the largest fountain or spring I ever saw, and doubt if it is not the largest in America known. This water boils up from under the rocks near the edge of the river and falls immediately into the river 8 feet, and keeps its color for half a mile, which is immensely clear and of a bluish cast.

We saw a gang of buffalo swimming the river above the falls, several of which were drawn into the rapids and with difficulty made shore half drowned. We killed one of those cows and took as much meat as we wished. There are immense herds of those animals in every direction.

This evening, one man, A. Willard, going for a load of meat at 170 yards distance on an island, was attacked by a white bear and was very near being caught. He was pursued within 40 yards of camp where I was with one man. I collected three others of the party and pursued the bear (who had pursued my track from a buffalo I had killed on the island at about 300 yards distance and chanced to meet Willard) for fear of his attacking one man, Colter, at the lower point of the island. Before we had gotten down, the bear had alarmed the man and pursued him into the water. At our approach, the bear retreated, and we relieved the man in the water.

Clark, June 18, 1805

Clark was right — Giant Springs, as it is now known, is the largest freshwater spring in America.

June 30, 1805, mile 2575

Portage Creek enters the Missouri among some rapids. While the river channel remains relatively stable in this area, the position of the rapids may move up or downstream over the years.

The expedition camped for two weeks about ¾ mile from here, below the falls and the rapids, while they hauled their equipment and provisions about 18 miles overland above the falls.

June 15, 1805, mile 2561

I now informed Captain Clark of my discoveries with respect to the most proper side for our portage, and of its great length, which I could not estimate at less than 16 miles.
Captain Clark determined to set out in the morning to examine the country, survey the portage, and discover the best route. As the distance was too great to think of transporting the canoes and baggage on the men's shoulders, we selected six men and ordered them to look out some timber this evening, and early in the morning to set about making a parcel of truck wheels in order to convey our canoes and baggage over the portage.

Lewis, June 16, 1805

We made a tongue to one of the truck wagons and proceeded on. The wind blew steadily from the southeast. We hoisted a sail in the largest canoe, which helped us as much as four men hauling at the cord with a harness. We passed through high, smooth, delightful plains. We saw a number of antelope and buffalo. Towards the evening, when we were within 3 miles of the upper camp, there came up a sudden violent thunder shower and rained amazingly hard for about 15 or 20 minutes, in which time the water stood on the ground over our moccasins. Our water being all gone and all the men thirsty, we drunk heartily out of the puddles.

Whitehouse, June 24, 1805,
portaging around the Great Falls

A fine morning. Captain Lewis, myself, and all the party except Sergeant Ordway, Guterich, and the interpreter and his wife, Sacagawea (who are left at camp to take care of the baggage), left across the portage with one canoe on truck wheels and loaded with a part of our baggage. I piloted through the plains to the camp I made at which place I intended the portage to end, which is 3 miles above the Medicine River.
We had great difficulty in getting on, as the axletree broke several times and the coupling tongues of the wheels, which were made of cottonwood and willow, the only wood except box elder that grow in this quarter. We got within half a mile of our intended camp much fatigued after dark. Our tongues broke and we took a load to the river on the men's backs, where we found a number of wolves which had destroyed a great part of our meat, which I had left at that place when I was up the day before yesterday.

Clark, June 22, 1805

The portage around Great Falls was much harder and took longer than Lewis and Clark had anticipated.

Lewis had designed and constructed an iron boat frame before leaving on the expedition. He planned to cover with it with elk skin and use it above the portage in place of the pirogue. They had left one pirogue behind at the Marias River and the other one at the foot of the portage. After it was finished, the leather boat leaked, primarily because there were no trees available to provide good sealant for the seams. Lewis thought he could have eventually made the boat work, but its construction had already delayed them a few days so he left it behind. Since they had no leather boat, they needed some canoes. This was a problem because there were no trees big enough for canoes near the top of the portage.

They sent a few men 8 miles upstream from the top of the portage to find some timber and build canoes. They built two canoes, one 25 and one 33 feet long. These were shorter than they wanted because of the lack of suitable trees. The rest of the party used the other four canoes to shuttle the "baggage" up to the canoe-building camp.

Lewis and Clark got to the Marias River on June 2, 1805. They finally got underway with the eight canoes on July 15, after exploring the options and ascending the Marias River, making the 18-mile portage, and building a couple of new canoes. It took them six weeks to go 55 miles, as the crow flies.

Their progress seems painfully slow; however, their goal was not only to get to the Pacific, but also to explore the territory along the way. They wrote dozens of pages of descriptions in this stretch alone. The complete journals that Lewis and Clark wrote on the expedition make up more than 2,000 typewritten pages.

Fields informed me that he had seen two white bear near the river, a few miles above. Attempting to get a shot at them he had stumbled upon a third, which immediately made at him, being only a few steps distant. In running in order to escape from the bear, he had leaped down a steep bank of the river onto a stony bar, where he fell, cut his hand, bruised his knees, and bent his gun. Fortunately for him, the bank hid him from the bear when he fell and by that means he had escaped. This man has been truly unfortunate with these bears; this is the second time he has narrowly escaped from them.

Lewis, June 25, 1805

The Montana Refinery in Great Falls gets its crude oil through a pipeline from Canada. The Great Falls air traffic controller asked us not to loiter when we flew by the refinery. Maybe our 70 mph speed seemed a little slow.

June 30, 1805, mile 2577

We launched the leather boat and found that it leaked a little. We corked, launched, and loaded the canoes, buried our truck wheels, and made a cache for a skin and a few papers I intend to leave here.

On trial, we found the leather boat would not answer without the addition of tar, which we had none. We had substituted coal tallow in its place to stop the seams, which would not answer as it separated from the skins when exposed to the water, and left the skins naked and seams exposed to the water. This failure of our favorite boat was a great disappointment to us, we having more baggage than our canoes would carry. We concluded to build canoes to carry them. There is no timber near our camp. I determined to proceed on up the river to a bottom in which our hunters reported were large trees.

Clark, July 9, 1805

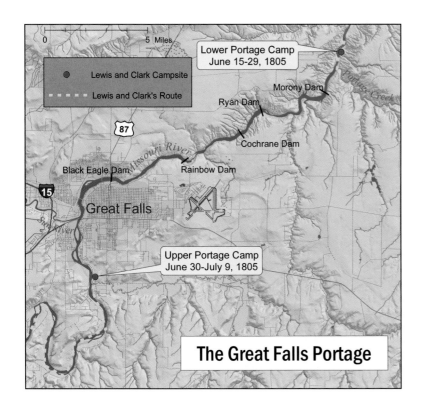

The Great Falls Portage

Lower Portage Camp
June 15-29, 1805

Morony Dam

Ryan Dam

Cochrane Dam

Black Eagle Dam

Rainbow Dam

Great Falls

Upper Portage Camp
June 30-July 9, 1805

Lewis and Clark Campsite

Lewis and Clark's Route

0   5 Miles

Missouri River

In the afternoon there arose a storm of hard wind and rain, and amazingly large hail at our camp. We measured and weighed some of them, and Captain Lewis made a bowl of ice punch of one of them. They were 7 inches in circumference and weighed 3 ounces. As luck would have it, we were all that stayed at this camp safe in a shelter, but we feel concerned about the men on the road.

Whitehouse, June 29, 1805

I took my servant and one man, Charbonneau our interpreter, and his squaw accompanied. Soon after I arrived at the falls, I perceived a cloud which appeared black and threatened immediate rain. I looked out for a shelter, but could see no place without being in great danger of being blown into the river if the wind should prove as turbulent as it is at some times.

About a quarter of a mile above the falls I observed a deep ravine, in which were shelving rocks under which we took shelter near the river. We placed our guns, the compass, etc., under a shelving rock on the upper side of the creek in a place which was very secure from rain.

The first shower was moderate, accompanied with a violent wind, the effects of which we did not feel. Soon after, a torrent of rain and hail fell more violent than ever I saw before. The rain fell like one volley of water falling from the heavens, and gave us time only to get out of the way of a torrent of water which was pouring down the hill into the river with the immense force tearing everything before it, taking with it large rocks and mud.

I took my gun and shot pouch in my left hand, and with the right scrambled up the hill, pushing the interpreter's wife (who had her child in her arms) before me. The interpreter himself was making attempts to pull up his wife by the hand, much scared and nearly without motion. We at length reached the top of the hill safe, where I found my servant in search of us, greatly agitated for our welfare.

Before I got to the bottom of the ravine, which was a flat, dry rock when I entered it, the water was up to my waist and wet my watch. I scarcely got out before it raised 10 feet deep with a torrent which was terrible to behold, and by the time I reached the top of the hill, there was at least 15 feet of water.

I directed the party to return to the camp at the run as fast as possible to get to our load where clothes could be gotten to cover the child, whose clothes were all lost, and the woman, who was but just recovering from a severe indisposition, and was wet and cold. I was fearful of a relapse. I caused her as also the others of the party to take a little spirits, which my servant had in a canteen. This revived them very much.

On arrival at the camp on the willow run, I met the party who had returned in great confusion to the run, leaving their loads in the plain, the hail and wind being so large and violent in the plains, and them [nearly] naked, they were much bruised and some nearly killed. One was knocked down three times, and others, without hats or anything on their heads, were bloody and complained very much. I refreshed them with a little grog.

Soon after, the run began to rise and rose six feet in a few minutes. I lost at the river in the torrent the large compass, an elegant fusee, tomahawk, umbrella, shot pouch and horn with powder and ball, moccasins, and the woman lost her child's bear, clothing, and bedding, etc. The compass is a serious loss, as we have no other large one. The plains are so wet that we can do nothing this evening, particularly as two deep ravines are between ourselves and the load.

Clark, June 29, 1805

July 10, 1805, mile 2600

Mosquitoes are extremely troublesome to me today, nor is a large black gnat less troublesome. It does not sting, but attacks the eye in swarms and compels us to brush them off or have our eyes filled with them.

Lewis, July 12, 1805

The expedition camped in this area and built two canoes. The white cone-shaped structure near the center of this photo in the plain is the Great Falls VOR, shown on the aviation chart to the right. A VOR transmits radio signals used for aviation navigation.

I passed a very extraordinary Indian lodge, or at least the frame of one. It was formed of sixteen large cottonwood poles, each about 50 feet long, and at their larger end, which rested on the ground, as thick as a man's body. These were arranged in a circular manner at bottom and equally distributed, except the omission of one on the east side which I suppose was the entrance to the lodge. The upper part of the poles are united in a common point above, and secured with large withes of willow brush. In the center of this fabric there were the remains of a large fire, and about the place the marks of about 80 leather lodges.

I knew not what was the intention or design of such a lodge, but certain I am that it was not designed for a dwelling of any one family. It was 216 feet in circumference at the base. It was most probably designed for some great feast, or a council house, or some great national concern.

Lewis, July 13, 1805

About 11 o'clock the men came up with the canoes and baggage. The distance by water was found to be 22 miles, and by land only 6 miles.

Gass, July 14, 1805

All hands that could work were employed about the canoes, which completed and launched this evening. The one was 25 feet and the other 33 feet in length, and about 3 feet wide. We have now the seats and oars to make and fit.

Lewis, July 14, 1805

Our canoes being so small, several of the men, Captain Lewis, and myself were compelled to walk on shore and cross the bends to keep up with the canoes.

Clark, July 15, 1805

July 16, 1805, mile 2638

Cascade, Montana is squeezed between the Missouri River and Interstate 15.

The expedition ascended the river here on July 15, 1805, their first full day on the water after the long portage around the Great Falls of the Missouri. They traveled almost 20 miles that day.

July 15, 1805, mile 2620

We arose very early this morning, assigned the canoes their loads, and had it put on board. We now found our vessels, eight in number, all heavy laden, notwithstanding our several deposits. Though it is true we have now a considerable stock of dried meat and grease. We find it extremely difficult to keep the baggage of many of our men within reasonable bounds. They will be adding bulky articles of but little use or value to them. At 10 a.m. we once more saw ourselves fairly underway, much to my joy and, I believe, that of every individual who composes the party.

Lewis, July 15, 1805

July 17, 1805, mile 2651

Interstate 15 and the BNSF Railroad follow the Missouri into the Rocky Mountains south of Great Falls, Montana. The expedition traveled twelve miles on July 17, 1805, a hard day's work. Today it takes ten minutes.

We set out early this morning and crossed the rapid at the island called Pine Rapid with some difficulty. The immense high precipices oblige all the party to pass and re-pass the river from one point to another. The river is confined in many places in a very narrow channel from 70 to 120 yards wide. Bottoms are narrow without timber and in many places the mountains approach on both sides.

I ascended a spur of the mountain which I found to be high and difficult of access, containing pitch pine and covered with grass. There was scarcely any game to be seen. I saw several ibex or mountain rams today.

Clark, July 17, 1805.

July 17, 1805, mile 2649

July 17, 1805, mile 2651

July 18, 1805, mile 2657

We proceeded on through the mountains, a very desert looking part of the country. Some of the knobs or peaks of these mountains are 700 or perhaps nearly 1,200 feet high, all rock, and though they are almost perpendicular, we saw mountain sheep on the very tops of them.
Gass, July 17, 1805

July 18, 1805, mile 2669

A rowboat plies the Missouri River
5 miles below Holter Lake.

We passed a considerable
river which falls in on the
starboard side, nearly as wide as
the Missouri. We call it
Dearborn's River, after the
Secretary of War.
    We thought it would be
prudent for a party to go ahead,
for fear our firing should alarm the
Indians and cause them to leave
the river and take to the
mountains for safety from their
enemies, who visit them through
this route. I determined to go
ahead with a small party a few
days and find the Snake Indians,
if possible. After breakfast I took
J. Fields, my servant, and
proceeded on.
    The country is so hilly that
we gained but little on the canoes
until in the evening, when I passed
over a mountain on an Indian
road, by which I cut off several
miles of the meanderings of the
river. The road, which passes the
mountain, is wide and appears to
have been dug in many places.

Clark, July 18, 1805

July 18, 1805, mile 2658

Muddy water from the
Dearborn River enters
the Missouri underneath
the Interstate 15 Bridge.

The muddy water from Little Prickly Pear Creek is visible in the Missouri two miles downstream from the mouth of the creek.

July 18, 1805, mile 2670

My feet are very much bruised and cut, walking over the flint and constantly stuck full of prickly pear thorns. I pulled out 17 by the light of the fire tonight.

Clark, July 19, 1805

Little Prickly Pear Creek, named Ordway's Creek by Lewis and Clark, joins the Missouri below Holter Dam.

July 18, 1805, mile 2672

July 18, 1805, mile 2674

Holter Lake extends through the "Gates of the Mountains" described by Lewis. The 125-foot Holter Dam was built in 1918.

The Gates of the Mountains is this majestic four-mile canyon formed by the Missouri. It is now a part of Lake Holter.

July 19, 1805, mile 2695

Whenever we get a view of the lofty summits of the mountains the snow presents itself, although we are almost suffocated in this confined valley with heat. The pine cedar and balsam fir grow on the mountains in irregular assemblages or spots, mostly high up on their sides and summits. This evening we entered much the most remarkable cliffs that we have yet seen. These cliffs rise from the water's edge on either side, perpendicularly to the height of about 1,200 feet.

Every object here wears a dark and gloomy aspect. The towering and projecting rocks in many places seem ready to tumble on us. The river appears to have forced its way through this immense body of solid rock for the distance of 5¾ miles, and where it makes its exit below has thrown on either side vast columns of rocks, mountains high. The river appears to have worn a passage just the width of its channel, or 150 yards. It is deep from side to side, nor is there in the first 3 miles of this distance a spot except one of a few yards in extent on which a man could rest the sole of his foot.

Several fine springs burst out at the water's edge from the interstices of the rocks. It happens fortunately that although the current is strong, it is not so much so but what it may be overcome with the oars, for there is here no possibility of using either the cord or setting pole.

It was late in the evening before I entered this place and was obliged to continue my route until sometime after dark before I found a place sufficiently large to encamp my small party. At length such a one occurred on the larboard side where we found plenty of lightwood and pitch pine. This rock is a black granite below and appears to be of a much lighter color above and from the fragments. I take it to be flint of a yellowish brown and light cream colored yellow.

From the singular appearance of this place I called it the Gates of the Rocky Mountains. The mountains are higher today than yesterday. We saw some bighorns and a few antelopes, also beaver and otter. The latter are now very plentiful. One of the men killed one of them today with a setting pole.

Lewis, July 19, 1805

July 19, 1805, mile 2697

Lewis and Clark wanted to meet with the Indians so they could barter for horses for the trip across the Rocky Mountains. They also hoped to get information and hire a guide. Because the Indians in this area did not have guns and generally fled at the sound of gunfire, the expedition's hunters may have been scaring them away.

July 19, 1805, mile 2696

Sacagawea Mountain rises 6,539 feet, east of the Gates of the Mountains.

At 6 a.m. the hills retreated from the river and the valley became wider than we have seen it since we entered the mountains. About 10 a.m. we saw the smoke arise as if the country had been set on fire up the valley of this creek about 7 miles distant. We were at a loss to determine whether it had been set on fire by the natives as a signal among themselves on discovering us, as is their custom, or whether it had been set on fire by Captain Clark and party accidentally. The first, however, proved to be the fact.

Lewis, July 20, 1805

July 20, 1805, mile 2707

The cause of this smoke I can't account for certainly, though I think it probable that the Indians have heard the shooting of the party below and set the prairies or valley on fire to alarm their camps, supposing our party to be a war party coming against them. I left signs to show the Indians if they should come on our trail that we were not their enemies.

The feet of the men with me are so stuck with prickly pear and cut with the stones that they were scarcely able to march at a slow gait this afternoon.

Clark, July 20, 1805

Hauser Dam is immediately above Lake Holter on the Missouri River. Hauser Lake, in turn, reaches almost to Canyon Ferry Dam a few more miles upstream.

The 225-foot Canyon Ferry Dam was completed in 1954. It is located about 15 miles east of Helena, Montana, a mile and a half downstream from the older dam it replaced.

July 21, 1805, mile 2724

York Bridge crosses Hauser Lake at Trout Creek, northeast of Helena, Montana.

> We set out early this morning and passed a bad rapid where the river enters the mountain about 1 mile from our camp of last evening. The cliffs are high and covered with fragments of broken rocks. The current is strong. We employed the tow rope principally and also the poles, as the river is not now so deep but rather wider and much more rapid. Our progress was therefore slow and laborious.
>
> *Lewis, July 21, 1805*

July 21, 1805, mile 2726

July 21, 1805, mile 2715

Cemetery Hill became Cemetery Island when the new Canyon Ferry Dam was built. The original Canyon Ferry Dam was built in 1898 between this island and the far shore in this photo. The old cemetery still remains on this island.

The river was divided into such a number of channels by both large and small Islands that I found it impossible to lay it down correctly, following one channel only in a canoe, and therefore walked on shore. I took the general courses of the river and, from the rising grounds, took a view of the islands and its different channels, which I laid down in conformity thereto on my chart.

There being but little timber to obstruct my view I could see its various meanders very satisfactorily. I passed through a large Island, which I found a beautiful level and fertile plain about 10 feet above the surface of the water and never overflown. On this Island I met with great quantities of a small onion about the size of a musket ball, and some even larger. They were white, crisp, and well flavored. I gathered about half a bushel of them before the canoes arrived. I halted the party for breakfast and the men also gathered considerable quantities of those onions.

While waiting for the canoes to arrive I killed an otter which sunk to the bottom on being shot, a circumstance unusual with that animal. The water was about 8 feet deep yet so clear that I could see it at the bottom. I swam in and obtained it by diving.

I halted the party here for dinner. The canoes had taken different channels through these islands and it was some time before they all came up. I placed my thermometer in a good shade, as was my custom, about 4 p.m. After dinner I set out without it and had proceeded near a mile before I recollected it. I sent Sergeant Ordway back for it. He found it and brought it on. The mercury stood at 80 degrees. This is the warmest day except one which we have experienced this summer.

The Indian woman recognizes the country and assures us that this is the river on which her relations live, and that the three forks are at no great distance. This piece of information has cheered the spirits of the party who now begin to console themselves with the anticipation of shortly seeing the head of the Missouri yet unknown to the civilized world.

Lewis, July 22, 1805

July 22, 1805, mile 2741

The expedition's route of July 22 is now underwater in Canyon Ferry Lake.

July 24, 1805, mile 2786

I fear every day that we shall meet with some considerable falls or obstruction in the river, notwithstanding the information of the Indian woman to the contrary who assures us that the river continues much as we see it. I can scarcely form an idea of a river running to great extent through such a rough mountainous country without having its stream intercepted by some difficult and dangerous rapids or falls.

We daily pass a great number of small rapids or riffles which descend one, two, or three feet in 150 yards, but we are rarely incommoded with fixed or standing rocks, and although strong rapid water, they are nevertheless quite practicable and by no means dangerous.

We saw many beaver and some otter today. The former dam up the small channels of the river between the islands and compel the river in these parts to make other channels. As soon as it has effected, that which was stopped by the beaver becomes dry and is filled up with mud, sand, gravel, and driftwood. The beaver is then compelled to seek another spot for his habitation, where he again erects his dam. Thus the river in many places among the clusters of islands is constantly changing the direction of such sluices as the beaver are capable of stopping, or of 20 yards in width. This animal in that way I believe to be very instrumental in adding to the number of islands with which we find the river crowded.

We observed a great number of snakes about the water of a brown uniform color, some black, and others speckled on the abdomen and striped with black and brownish yellow on the back and sides. The first of these is the largest, being about 4 feet long. The second is of that kind mentioned yesterday, and the last is much like the garter snake of our country and about its size. None of these species are poisonous. I examined their teeth and found them innocent. They all appear to be fond of the water, to which they fly for shelter immediately on being pursued.

We saw much sign of elk but met with none of them. From the appearance of bones and excrement of old date the buffalo sometimes straggle into this valley, but there is no fresh sign of them and I begin to think that our harvest of white puddings is at an end, at least until our return to the buffalo country.

Our trio of pests still invade and obstruct us on all occasions, these are the mosquitoes, eye gnats, and prickly pears, equal to any three curses that ever poor Egypt labored under, except the Mohammedan yoke. The men complain of being much fatigued. Their labor is excessively great. I occasionally encourage them by assisting in the labor of navigating the canoes, and have learned to push a tolerable good pole, in their phrase.

Lewis, July 24, 1805

Toston, Montana

We saw some antelope, of which we killed one. These animals appear now to have collected again in small herds. Several females with their young and one or two males compose the herd usually. Some males are yet solitary, or two perhaps together, scattered over the plains, which they seem invariably to prefer to the woodlands. If they happen accidentally in the woodlands and are alarmed, they run immediately to the plains, seeming to place a just confidence in their superior fleetness and bottom.

We killed a couple of young geese which are very abundant and fine, but as they are but small game to subsist a party on of our strength, I have forbid the men from shooting at them as it wastes a considerable quantity of ammunition and time.

Lewis, July 25, 1805

Here the hills, or rather mountains, again recede from the river and the valley again widens to the extent of several miles, with wide and fertile bottom lands covered with grass and in many places a fine turf of greensward. The high lands are thin, meager soil covered with dry low sedge and a species of grass, also dry, the seeds of which are armed with a long, twisted, hard beard at the upper extremity. The lower point is a sharp subulate, firm point, beset at its base with little stiff bristles standing with their points in a contrary direction to the subulate point, to which they answer as a barb and serve also to press it forward when once entered a small distance.

These barbed seeds penetrate our moccasins and leather leggings and give us great pain until they are removed. My poor dog suffers with them excessively. He is constantly biting and scratching himself as if in a rack of pain.

Lewis, July 26, 1805

July 26, 1805, mile 2811

July 26, 1805, mile 2811

The new and the old railroads cross at Lombard, Montana.

July 26, 1805, mile 2826

At 4 o'clock we proceeded on through the valley, passed a creek on the south side, and having gone some 18 miles and a half, we encamped on the same side, where a small mountain comes into the river.

Gass, July 26, 1805

This rock is probably the "small mountain" where the expedition camped on July 26, 1805. Lewis describes it as a rock in the center of a bend, while Gass calls it a small mountain that comes into the river.

We set out at an early hour and proceeded on, but slowly. The current is still so rapid that the men are in a continual state of their utmost exertion to get on, and they begin to weaken fast from this continual state of violent exertion.

At the distance of 1 ¾ miles, the river was again closely hemmed in by high cliffs of a solid limestone rock which appears to have tumbled or sunk in the same manner of those I described yesterday. The limestone appears to be of an excellent quality of deep blue color when fractured, and of a light lead color where exposed to the weather. It appears to be of a very fine grain, the fracture like that of marble. We saw a great number of bighorn on those cliffs.

Lewis, July 27, 1805

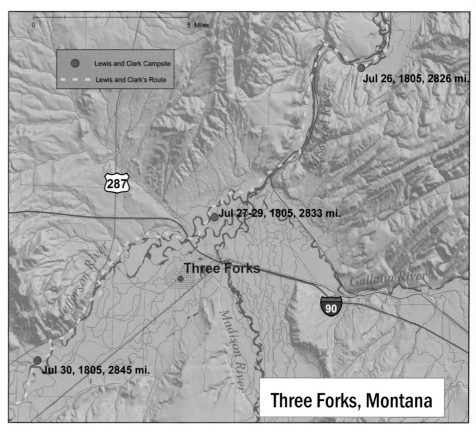

Three Forks, Montana

This map of the Three Forks area illustrates some of the challenge in the expedition's river navigation.

July 27, 1805, mile 2830

The Holcim cement plant in Trident, Montana, utilizes some of the limestone that Lewis described as "excellent quality."

Lewis, Arriving at the Three Forks of the Missouri

We arrived at 9 a.m. at the junction of the southeast fork of the Missouri. The country opens suddenly to extensive and beautiful plains and meadows, which appear to be surrounded in every direction with distant and lofty mountains. Supposing this to be the three forks of the Missouri, I halted the party on the larboard shore for breakfast and walked up the southeast fork about half a mile. I ascended the point of a high limestone cliff from whence I commanded a most perfect view of the neighboring country.

From this point I could see the southeast fork at about 7 miles. It is rapid

This is the "Three Forks of the Missouri" viewed from the east. Lewis climbed the cliff on the right of the photo, next to the river, to make his observations. The flat, raised area near the center of the photo is the 25-foot high limestone rock that he thought would make an ideal site for a fort. This is now part of the Missouri Headwaters State Park.

July 27, 1805, mile 2832

and about 70 yards wide. Throughout the distance I saw it. It passes through a smooth, extensive green meadow of fine grass in its course, meandering in several streams. The largest of these passes near the larboard hills, of which the one I stand on is the extremity in this direction. A high, wide, and extensive plain succeeds the meadow and extends back several miles from the river on the starboard side, with the range of mountains up the larboard side of the middle fork.

A large spring arises in this meadow about a quarter of a mile from the southeast fork, into which it discharges itself on the starboard side, about 400 paces above me. From east to south, between the southeast and middle forks, a distant range of lofty mountains ran their snowclad tops above the irregular and broken mountains which lie adjacent to this beautiful spot.

The extreme point to which I could see the southeast fork bore S 65° E, distance 7 miles, as before observed. Between the middle and southeast forks, near their junction with the southwest fork, there is a handsome site for a fortification. It consists of a limestone rock of an oblong form. Its sides are perpendicular and about 25 feet high, except at the extremity towards the middle fork where it ascends gradually, and like the top is covered with a fine turf of greensward. The top is level and contains about one acre. The rock rises from the level plain as if it had been designed for some such purpose.

The extreme point to which I can see the bottom and meandering of the middle fork bears S 15° E, distance about 14 miles. Here it turns to the right around a point of a high plain and disappears to my view. Its bottoms are several miles in width and like that of the southeast fork form one smooth and beautiful green meadow. It is also divided into several streams. Between this and the southwest fork there is an extensive plain which appears to extend up both those rivers many miles and back to the mountains.

The extreme point to which I can see the southwest fork bears S 30° W, distance about 12 miles. This stream passes through a country similar to the other two, and is more divided and serpentine in its course than either of the others. It also possesses abundantly more timber in its bottoms. The timber here consists of the narrow-leafed cottonwood almost entirely, but little box elder or sweet willow. The underbrush is thick and as heretofore described in this quarter of the Missouri.

A range of high mountains at a considerable distance appears to reach from south to west and are partially covered with snow. The country to the right of the southwest fork, like that to the left of the southeast fork, is high, broken, and mountainous, as is that also down the Missouri behind us, through which these three rivers, after assembling their united force at this point, seem to have forced a passage. These bottomlands, though not more than 8 or 9 feet above the water, seem never to overflow.

July 27, 1805, mile 2831

The Gallatin River joins the Missouri just downstream of the junction of the other two forks.

Believing this to be an essential point in the geography of this western part of the continent, I determined to remain at all events until I obtained the necessary data for fixing its latitude and longitude. After fixing my camp, I had the canoes all unloaded and the baggage stowed away and securely covered on shore, and then permitted several men to hunt.

I walked down to the middle fork and examined and compared it with the southwest fork, but could not satisfy myself which was the largest stream of the two. In fact, they appeared as if they had been cast in the same mold, there being no difference in character or size.

Therefore to call either of these streams the Missouri would be giving it a preference which its size dose not warrant, as it is not larger then the other. They are each 90 yards wide.

Below the three forks as we passed this morning I observed many collections of the mud nests of the small martin attached to the smooth face of the limestone rocks sheltered by projections of the same rock above. Our hunters returned this evening with 6 deer, 3 otters and a muskrat. They informed me that they had seen great numbers of antelopes, and much sign of beaver, otter, deer, elk, etc.

We begin to feel considerable anxiety with respect to the Snake Indians. If we do not find them, or

Viewed from the north, this is where the Madison River, in the upper part of the photo, meets the Jefferson, coming in from the right. Lewis and Clark couldn't determine which river was the primary river, so they decided that this was the end of the Missouri and named the three forks the Jefferson, the Madison, and the Gallatin. The three rivers still bear those names. They followed the Jefferson River, the westernmost fork.

some other nation who has horses, I fear the successful issue of our voyage will be very doubtful, or at all events much more difficult in its accomplishment.

We are now several hundred miles within the bosom of this wild and mountainous country, where game may rationally be expected shortly to become scarce and subsistence precarious without any information with respect to the country; we not knowing how far these mountains continue, or where to direct our course to pass them to advantage, or where intercept a navigable branch of the Columbia. Even were we on such a course, the probability is that we should not find any timber within these mountains large enough for canoes, if we judge from the portion of the mountains through which we have passed.

However, I still hope for the best, and intend taking a tramp myself in a few days to find these yellow gentlemen, if possible. My two principal consolations are that from our present position it is impossible that the southwest fork can head with the waters of any other river but the Columbia, and that if any Indians can subsist in the form of a nation in these mountains with the means they have of acquiring food, we can also subsist.

Lewis, July 27, 1805

July 27, 1805, mile 2832

Lewis wrote that it looked like these rivers were cast from the same mold, there being no difference in character or size. The day we flew over, the Jefferson River was muddier than the Madison.

From this view to the southwest it appears that the Madison and Jefferson rivers are about the same size, and neither one is very straight. The Gallatin River is in the foreground coming in from the left, and the fork between the Madison and the Jefferson is near the center of the picture. The town of Three Forks, Montana is visible in the distance.

July 27, 1805, mile 2832

Our present camp is precisely on the spot that the Snake Indians were encamped at the time the Minetares of the Knife River first came in sight of them five years since. From hence they retreated about 3 miles up the Jefferson River and concealed themselves in the woods. The Minetares pursued, attacked them, killed four men, four women, and a number of boys; and made prisoners of all the females and four boys. Sacagawea, our Indian woman, was one of the female prisoners taken at the time, though I cannot discover that she shows any emotion of sorrow in recollecting this event, or of joy in being again restored to her native country. If she has enough to eat and a few trinkets to wear, I believe she would be perfectly content anywhere.

We set out at eight o'clock and proceeded on 13 ½ miles up the north fork. The river is very rapid and shoaly. The channel is entirely coarse gravel. There are many islands and a number of channels in different directions through the bottom.

Clark, July 30, 1805

July 30, 1805, mile 2840

Highway 287 squeezes between the Jefferson River and a mountain, west of Three Forks.

This bridge crosses the Jefferson River near Willow Creek, Montana. Lewis was walking along the river in this area on July 30, 1805. When he couldn't find the rest of the party, he shot a duck, cooked it over a driftwood fire, and camped alone. He said he "should have had a comfortable night's lodge but for the mosquitoes."

July 31, 1805, mile 2846

July 31, 1805, mile 2854

Parallel railroads accompany the Jefferson River into the mountains. On July 31, Lewis decided to take three men the following day and walk ahead in search of the Snake or Shoshone Indians.

August 1, 1805, mile 2865

This old house is not far from the expedition's July 31 campsite.

Nothing was killed today, and our fresh meat is out. When we have plenty of fresh meat I find it impossible to make the men take any care of it, or use it with the least frugality, though I expect that necessity will shortly teach them this art. The mountains on both sides of the river at no great distance are very lofty.

We have a lame crew just now, two with tumors or bad boils on various parts of them, one with a bad stone bruise, one with his arm accidentally dislocated but, fortunately, well replaced, and a fifth has strained his back by slipping and falling backwards on the gunwale of the canoe.

Lewis, July 31, 1805

August 1, 1805, mile 2865

Lewis and three others left the main party to search for Indians shortly before they reached this mountain.

August 1, 1805, mile 2869

August 1, 1805, mile 2870

The river, the highway, and the railroad share the same route through the 9 miles of "very high mountain."

August 1, 1805, mile 2870

Captain Lewis left me at 8 o'clock, just below the place I entered a very high mountain which jutted its tremendous cliffs on either side for 9 miles. The rocks are ragged, some very dark and the other part very light rock. The light rock is sandstone. The water is swift and very shoaly. I killed an Ibex [bighorn sheep], on which the whole party dined. After passing through the mountain we entered a wide, extensive valley of from four to 8 miles wide, and very level. The river widens and spreads into small channels. The river is so rapid that the greatest exertion is required by all to get the boats on. I sent J. and R. fields to hunt this evening. They killed five deer.

Clark, August 1, 1805

August 2, 1805, mile 2883

This is the "wide, extensive valley" Clark described, near the August 1 campsite. The town of Whitehall appears in the distance, with Interstate 90 to its right.

Mountains border the east side of the Beaverhead Valley near Silver Star, Montana.

August 3, 1805, mile 2899

I walked on shore and killed a deer. In my walk I saw a fresh track, which I took to be an Indian from the shape of the foot as the toes turned in. I think it probable that this Indian spied our fires and came to a situation to view us from the top of a small knob on the larboard side. The river is more rapid and shoaly than yesterday. One man killed a large panther on the shore. We are obliged to haul the canoes over the shoals in many places where the islands are numerous and the bottoms shoaly.

Clark, August 3, 1805

August 3, 1805, mile 2892

August 3, 1805, mile 2903

Almost 200 years later, the Jefferson River still has many islands and shoals.

The navigation of eight large canoes up this part of the river was not easy. In this photo, the Wisdom River, now called the Big Hole River, ascends to the right along the border of the brown and green country. The Jefferson River, now called the Beaverhead beyond this point, branches off to the left. Today the Wisdom River meets the Jefferson about 2 miles downstream from the 1805 junction.

August 5, 1805, mile 2925

The river continued to be crowded with islands, shoaly, rapid, and clear. The method we are compelled to take to get on is fatiguing and laborious in the extreme. We haul the canoes over the rapids, which succeed each other every 200 or 300 yards, and between, the water is rapid and we are obliged to tow. We walk on stones the whole day, except when we have poling. The men are wet all day with sore feet.

Clark, August 4, 1805

Lewis left a note for Clark on a pole at the fork between the Jefferson and the Wisdom rivers, but beavers took the pole and the note before Clark got there. The note said to turn left. Clark turned right.

The mouth of the Wisdom River is on the right of this map, near Twin Bridges. Clark and the main party traveled several miles up the Wisdom River before learning of the mistake.

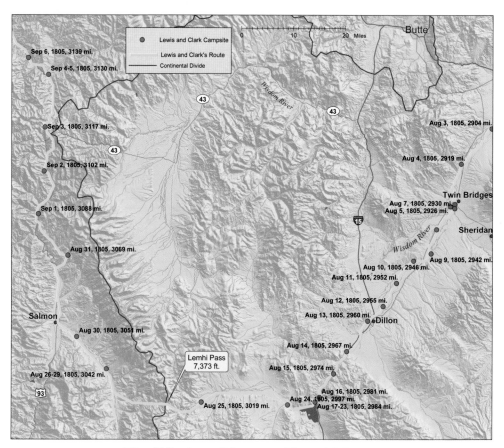

The Wisdom River and Lemhi Pass

The river is straight and much more rapid than yesterday. We proceeded on with great difficulty from the rapidity of the current and the innumerable rapids we had to encounter. We passed the mouth of a principal fork which falls in on the larboard side. This fork is about the size of the starboard one, with less water rather not too rapid. Its course, as far as can be seen, is southeast, and appears to pass between two mountains. The northwest fork being the one most in our course, i.e. S 25° W as far as I can see, determined me to take this fork as the principal and most proper.

We ascended this fork about 1 mile and encamped on an island which had been lately overflown and was wet. We raised our beds on bushes. We passed a part of the river above the forks which was divided and scattered through the willows in such a manner as to render it difficult to pass through for a quarter of a mile. We were obliged to cut our way through the willows. The men are much fatigued from their excessive labors in hauling the canoes over the rapids, etc., and are very weak, being in the water all day.

Clark, August 5, 1805

The rapids on Wisdom River are not difficult by today's kayaking standards, but Lewis and Clark were in very large canoes, and they were going up the river rather than down.

Clark and the main party arrived at the confluence of the two rivers where I had left the note. This note had unfortunately been placed on a green pole, which the beaver had cut and carried off together with the note. The possibility of such an occurrence never once occurred to me when I placed it on the green pole. This accident deprived Captain Clark of any information with respect to the country, and supposing that the rapid fork was most in the direction which was proper to pursue, or west, he took that stream and ascended it with much difficulty about a mile. The men were so much fatigued today that they wished much that navigation was at an end that they might go by land.

Lewis, August 5, 1805

August 5, 1805, mile 2923

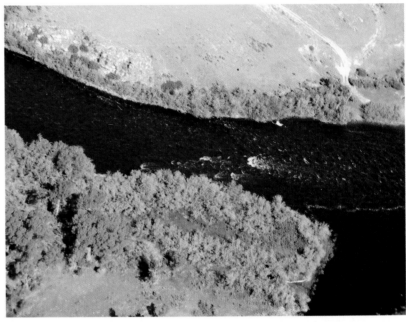

We proceeded on with much difficulty and fatigue over rapids and stones. The river is about 40 or 50 yards wide, much divided by islands and narrow bayous. We came to at a low bluff on the starboard side for breakfast. During the time of breakfast, Drouillard came to me from Captain Lewis and informed me that they had explored both forks for 30 or 40 miles and that the one we were ascending was impracticable much further up, and turned immediately to the north. The middle fork, he reported, was gentle and after a short distance turned to the southwest, and that all the Indian roads lead up the middle fork.

This report determined me to take the middle fork. Accordingly, we dropped down to the forks where I met with Captain Lewis and party. Captain Lewis had left a letter on a pole in the forks informing me what he had discovered, the course of the rivers, etc. This letter was cut down by the beaver, as it was on a green pole, and carried off. Three skins which were left on a tree were taken off by the panthers or wolves.

In descending to the point, one canoe struck and turned on a rapid and sunk, and wet everything which was in her. This misfortune obliged us to halt at the forks and dry those articles. One other canoe nearly turned over, filled half full of water, and wet our medicine and some goods, corn, etc. Several hunters went out to day and killed a young elk, antelope, and 3 deer. One man, Shannon, did not return tonight.

Clark, August 6, 1805

August 6, 1805, mile 2928

August 6, 1805, mile 2928

The Twin Bridges Airport is near the 1805 junction of the Wisdom and Jefferson rivers. We stopped here for a few minutes to warm up.

One of their canoes had just overset and all the baggage wet, the medicine box, among other articles, and several articles lost. A shot pouch and horn with all the implements for one rifle were lost and never recovered. I walked down to the point where I waited their return. On their arrival I found that two other canoes had filled with water and wet their cargoes completely.

Whitehouse had been thrown out of one of the canoes as she swung in a rapid current, and the canoe had rubbed him and pressed him to the bottom as she passed over him. Had the water been two inches shallower it must inevitably have crushed him to death.

Lewis, August 6, 1805

I was in the stern when she swung and jumped out to prevent her from turning over, but the current took her around so rapidly that I caught my leg under her and lamed me, as I was near breaking my leg. I lost my shot pouch, powder horn full of powder, a bunch of thread, and some moccasins. The remainder of the loading was saved.

Whitehouse, August 6, 1805

As Lewis observed, the river is deeper here and the current not as swift, but the river is very crooked with bends within bends.

August 8, 1805, mile 2932

We dispatched Rueben Fields in search of Shannon. Our stores were now so much exhausted that we could proceed with one canoe less. We therefore drew out one of them into a thicket of brush and secured her in such manner that the water could not take her off, should the river rise to the height where she is.

Lewis, August 7, 1805

Shannon had been dispatched up the rapid fork to hunt by Captain Clark, before he met with Drouillard and learnt of his mistake in the rivers. When he returned, he sent Drouillard in search of Shannon, but Drouillard rejoined us this evening and reported that he had been several miles up the river and could find nothing of him. We had the trumpet sounded and fired several guns, but Shannon did not join us this evening. I am fearful he is lost again. This is the same man who was separated from us 15 days as we came up the Missouri, and subsisted 9 days of that time on grapes only.

Lewis, August 6, 1805

August 8, 1805, mile 2932

We set out at sunrise and continued our route up the river, which we find much more gentle and deep than below the entrance of the Wisdom River. It is from 35 to 45 yards wide, very crooked, with many short bends constituting large and general bends. Although we travel briskly and a considerable distance, it takes us only a few miles on our general course or route.

I observe a considerable quantity of the buffalo clover in the bottoms. There is sunflower, flax, greensward, thistle, and several species of rye grass, some of which rise to the height of 3 or 4 feet. There is a grass also with a soft, smooth leaf that bears its seeds very much like the timothy, but does not grow very luxuriant or appear as if it would answer so well as the common timothy for meadows. I preserved some of its seeds, which are now ripe, thinking perhaps it might answer better if cultivated, and at all events is at least worth the experiment.

At noon, Rueben Fields arrived and reported that he had been up the Wisdom River some miles above where it entered the mountain, and could find nothing of Shannon. He had killed a deer and an antelope. There are great quantities of beaver, otter, and muskrats in these rivers. We use the setting poles today almost altogether. We encamped on the larboard side where there was but little timber. We were obliged to use willow brush for fuel. The rosebushes and briars were very thick.

Lewis, August 8 1805

August 8, 1805, mile 2937

The Jefferson River, now called the Beaverhead River in this area, travels many miles to make a few linear miles.

The river is very crooked, much divided by islands, shallow, rocky in many places, and very rapid; insomuch that I have my doubts whether the canoes could get on or not, or if they do, it must be with a great deal of labor.

Lewis, August 9, 1805

August 9, 1805, mile 2941

An old river channel shows up in this field, winding around just as much as today's channel.

This is the rock Sacagawea recognized as Beaverhead Rock.

August 10, 1805, mile 2944

The Indian woman recognized the point of a high plain to our right which she informed us was not very distant from the summer retreat of her nation on a river beyond the mountains which runs to the west. This hill she says her nation calls the beaver's head, from a conceived resemblance of its figure to the head of that animal. She assures us that we shall either find her people on this river or on the river immediately west of its source, which, from its present size, cannot be very distant.

As it is now all important with us to meet with those people as soon as possible, I determined to proceed tomorrow with a small party to the source of the principal stream of this river and pass the mountains to the Columbia, and down that river, until I find the Indians. In short, it is my resolution to find them, or some others who have horses, if it should cause me a trip of one month.

Lewis, August 8, 1805

Shannon, the man whom we lost on the Wisdom River, joined us, having returned to the forks and pursued us up after pursuing the Wisdom River one day. Captain Lewis and three men set out after breakfast to examine the river above, find a portage, if possible, and find the Snake Indians.

Clark, August 9, 1805

Lewis, walking ahead, traveled thirty miles on his second day out. The main party was struggling to make 4 to 7 miles per day up this shallow river.

August 14, 1805, mile 2965

We passed several large islands and three small ones. The river is much more shoaly than below, which obliges us to haul the canoes over those shoals which succeed each other at short intervals. This is immensely laborious. The men are much fatigued and weakened by being continually in the water drawing canoes over the shoals. We encamped on the larboard side. The men complain very much of the immense labor they are obliged to undergo and wish much to leave the river. I pacify them. The weather is cool. There is nothing to eat but venison. The hunters killed three deer today.

Clark, August 12, 1805

August 11, 1805, mile 2950

At about 3 miles we came to a very large prairie island which is 3,000 miles from the Wood River or the mouth of the Missouri, so we call it 3,000 Mile Island. We took up the left side of it and had to haul over several shoal places.

Whitehouse, August 11, 1805

A farmer applies fertilizer or herbicide to a pasture in the bottomland of the Beaverhead (or Jefferson) River, in the area of 3,000 Mile Island. The river has moved around since 1805 and 3,000 Mile Island is no longer an island.

August 14, 1805, mile 2967

Six lanes of highway, two railroad tracks, and a river divide the mountains at Rattlesnake Cliffs, 7 miles southwest of Dillon, Montana on Interstate 15.

I saw several bald eagles and two large, white-headed fishing hawks. Both these birds were the same common to our country. From the number of rattlesnakes about the cliffs at which we halted, we call them the Rattlesnake Cliffs.

Lewis, August 10, 1805

On August 14, Clark and the main party went "7 miles to the gap of the mountains at Rattlesnake Cliffs where the river enters the mountains, the same being 16 miles by the meanders of the river." They camped near Rattlesnake Cliffs. Lewis had passed here four days earlier. On the 14th he was on the Lemhi River with the Indians he had met the day before, over the Continental Divide and about 70 miles ahead.

The morning being cold and the men stiff, I determined to take breakfast at the place we encamped. We set out at 7 o'clock and proceeded on. The river is very crooked and rapid as below. Some few trees are on the borders near the mountain. The river near the mountain is one continued rapid, which requires great labor to push and haul the canoes up. We encamped on the larboard side near the place the river passes through the mountain.

I checked our interpreter for striking his woman at their dinner. Several men have hurt themselves pushing up the canoes. I am obliged to use a pole occasionally.

Clark, August 14, 1805

August 15, 1805, mile 2973

The expedition camped in this area on August 15, about 6 miles below Clark Canyon Reservoir.

Captain Clark was near being bitten by a rattlesnake which was between his legs as he was standing on the shore fishing. He killed it and shot several others this afternoon.

Whitehouse, August 15, 1805

It is easy to understand that the men "suffered excessively with fatigue," when you consider the effort required to drag seven large canoes up this river.

August 16, 1805, mile 2976

Captain Clark passed between low and rugged mountains which had a few pine trees distributed over them. The cliffs are formed of limestone and a hard black rock intermixed. There are no trees on the river. The bottoms are narrow, and the river is crooked, shallow, shoaly, and rapid. The water is as cold as that of the best springs in our country. The men, as usual, suffered excessively with fatigue and the coldness of the water to which they were exposed for hours together.

Captain Clark was very near being bitten twice today by rattlesnakes. The Indian woman also narrowly escaped. They caught a number of fine trout. Captain Clark killed a buck, which was the only game killed today. The venison has an uncommon bitter taste which is unpleasant. I presume it proceeds from some article of their food, perhaps the willow, on the leaves of which they feed very much. They encamped this evening on the larboard side near a few cottonwood trees, about which there were the remains of several old Indian brush lodges.

Lewis, August 15, 1805

At the narrows I ascended a mountain, from the top of which I could see that the river forked near me. The left hand appeared the largest and bore southeast. The right passed from the west through an extensive valley. I could see but three small trees in any direction from the top of this mountain.

Clark, July 16, 1805

The members of the expedition also caught "many fine trout" in this area.

The 147-foot Clark Canyon Dam was completed in 1963. From the mouth of the Missouri to Camp Fortunate, now underwater behind the dam, the expedition ascended more than 5,000 vertical feet by river.

August 17, 1805, mile 2983

Clark Canyon Reservoir now covers the fork in the river of 1805. This photo was taken looking to the southwest. The southeast fork, now called Red Rock River, passed to the left of the island. The west fork that Lewis and Clark took, now called Medicine Creek, passed to the right of the island.

Lewis and Clark camped at the fork in the river, and called it Camp Fortunate. This is where they left their canoes, cached supplies for their return trip, and took up horses. The expedition camped here from August 17 to 23, 1805, along with some of the Shoshone Indians. These Indians had never seen white people before meeting Lewis a few days before.

Clark Meets the Indians

A fair, cold morning, wind southwest, the thermometer at 42 degrees at sunrise. We set out at 7 o'clock and proceeded on to the forks. I had not proceeded on 1 mile before I saw at a distance several Indians on horseback coming towards me. The interpreter and squaw who were before me at some distance danced for the joyful sight, and she made signs to me that they were her nation. As I approached nearer them, I discovered one of Captain Lewis's party with them dressed in their dress. They met me with great signs of joy. As the canoes were proceeding on nearly opposite me, I turned with those people and joined Captain Lewis who had camped with 16 of those Snake Indians at the forks 2 miles in advance.

Those Indians sung all the way to their camp, where the others had provided a kind of shade of willows stuck up in a circle. The three chiefs with Captain Lewis met me with great cordiality, embraced, and took a seat on a white robe. The main chief immediately tied to my hair six small pieces of shells resembling pearl, which are highly valued by those people and are procured from the nations residing near the sea coast. We then smoked in their fashion without shoes and without much ceremony and form.

Captain Lewis informed me he found those people on the Columbia River about 40 miles from the forks. At that place there was a large camp of them. He had persuaded those with him to come and see that what he said was the truth. They had been under great apprehension all the way, for fear of their being deceived. The great chief of this nation proved to be the brother of

August 24, 1805, mile 2985

the woman with us, and is a man of influence, sense, and easy and reserved manners. He appears to possess a great deal of Sincerity.

The canoes arrived and were unloaded. Everything appeared to astonish those people, the appearance of the men, their arms, the canoes, the clothing, my black servant, and the sagacity of Captain Lewis's dog. We spoke a few words to them in the evening respecting our route, intentions, our want of horses, etc., and gave them a few presents and medals. We made a number of inquiries of those people about the Columbia River, the country, game, etc. The account they gave us was very unfavorable, that the river abounded in immense falls, one particularly much higher than the falls of the Missouri, at that place the mountains closed so close that it was impracticable to pass, that the ridge continued on each side of perpendicular cliffs impenetrable, and that no deer, elk, or any game was to be found in that country. Added to that, they informed us that there was no timber on the river sufficiently large to make small canoes.

This information, if true, is alarming. I determined to go in advance and examine the country, to see if those difficulties presented themselves in the gloomy picture in which they painted them, to see if the river was practicable, and to see if I could find timber to build canoes. Those ideas and plans appeared to be agreeable to Captain Lewis's ideas on this point, and I selected 11 men, directed them to pack up their baggage, complete themselves with ammunition, take each an ax and such tools as will be suitable to build canoes, and be ready to set out at 10 o'clock tomorrow morning. Those people were greatly pleased.

Our hunters killed three deer & an antelope which were eaten in a short time. The Indians, being so harassed and compelled to move about in those rugged mountains that they are half starved, are living at this time on berries and roots which they gather in the plains. Those people are not beggarly but generous. Only one has asked me for anything, and he for powder.

Clark, August 17, 1805

This island was a hill near the fork in the river when Lewis and Clark were here.

Lewis's Impressions of the Shoshones

From what has been said of the Shoshones, it will be readily perceived that they live in a wretched state of poverty. Yet notwithstanding their extreme poverty, they are not only cheerful but even gay, and fond of gaudy dress and amusements. Like most other Indians they are great egotists and frequently boast of heroic acts which they never performed. They are also fond of games of risk. They are frank, communicative, fair in dealing, generous with the little they possess, extremely honest, and by no means beggarly.

Each individual is his own sovereign master, and acts from the dictates of his own mind, the authority of the chief being nothing more than mere admonition, supported by the influence which the propriety of his own exemplary conduct may have acquired him in the minds of the individuals who compose the band. The title of chief is not hereditary, nor can I learn that there is any ceremony of installment or other epoch in the life of a chief from which his title as such can be dated. In fact, every man is a chief, but all have not an equal influence on the minds of the other members of the community, and he who happens to enjoy the greatest share of confidence is the principal chief.

The Shoshones may be estimated at about 100 warriors, and about three times that number of women and children. They have more children among them than I expected to have seen among a people who procure subsistence with such difficulty. There are but few very old persons, nor did they appear to treat those with much tenderness or respect. The man is the sole proprietor of his wives and daughters, and can barter or dispose of either as he thinks proper. A plurality of wives is common among them, but these are not generally sisters as with the Minetares & Mandans, but are purchased of different fathers.

The father frequently disposes of his infant daughters in marriage to men who are grown or to men who have sons for whom they think proper to provide wives. The compensation given in such cases usually consists of horses or mules, which the father receives at the time of contract and converts to his own use. The girl remains with her parents until she is conceived to have obtained the age of puberty, which with them is considered to be about the age of 13 or 14 years. The female at this age is surrendered to her sovereign lord and husband agreeably to contract, and with her is frequently restored by the father quite as much as he received in the first instance in payment for his daughter; but this is discretionary with the father.

Sacagawea had been thus disposed of before she was taken by the Minetares, or had arrived to the years of puberty. The husband was yet living with this band. He was more than double her age and had two other wives. He claimed her as his wife, but said that as she had had a child by another man, who was Charbonneau, that he did not want her.

They seldom correct their children, particularly the boys, who soon become masters of their own acts. They give as a reason that it cows and breaks the spirit of the boy to whip him, and that he never recovers his independence of mind after he is grown.

They treat their women but with little respect, and compel them to perform every species of drudgery. The women collect the wild fruits and roots, attend to the horses or assist in that duty, cook, dress the skins and make all their apparel, collect wood and make their fires, arrange and form their lodges, and, when they travel, pack the horses and take charge of all the baggage. In short, the man does little else except attend his horses, hunt, and fish. The man considers himself degraded if he is compelled to walk any distance, and if he is so unfortunately poor as only to possess two horses, he rides the best himself and leaves the woman, or women if he has more than one, to transport their baggage and children on the other, and to walk if the horse is unable to carry the additional weight of their persons.

The chastity of their women is not held in high estimation. The husband will, for a trifle, barter the companion of his bed for a night, or longer if he conceives the reward adequate, though they are not so importunate that we should caress their women as the Sioux were. Some of their women appear to be held more sacred than in any nation we have seen.

I have requested the men to give them no cause of jealousy by having connection with their women without their knowledge, which with them, strange as it may seem, is considered as disgraceful to the husband as clandestine connections of a similar kind are among civilized nations. To prevent this mutual exchange of good offices altogether, I know it impossible to effect, particularly on the part of our young men whom some months abstinence have made very polite to those tawny damsels. No evil has yet resulted and I hope will not from these connections.

Notwithstanding the late loss of horses which this people sustained by the Minetares, the stock of the band may be very safely estimated at 700, of which they are perhaps about 40 colts and half that number of mules.

Lewis, August 19, 1805

Cameahwait, literally translated, is one who never walks. He told me that his nation had also given him another name by which he was signalized as a warrior, which was *Too-et'-te-can'-e* or black gun. These people have many names in the course of their lives, particularly if they become distinguished characters, for it seems that every important event by which they happen to distinguish themselves entitles them to claim another name, which is generally selected by themselves and confirmed by the nation.

Those distinguishing acts are killing and scalping an enemy, killing a white bear, leading a party to war who happen to be successful either in destroying their enemies or robbing them of their horses, or individually stealing the horses of an enemy. These are considered acts of equal heroism among them, and that of killing an enemy without scalping him is considered of no importance. In fact, the whole honor seems to be founded in the act of scalping, for if a man happens to slay a dozen of his enemies in action and others get the scalps or first lay their hand on the dead person, the honor is lost to him who killed them and devolves on those who scalp or first touch them.

Among the Shoshones, as well as all the Indians of America, bravery is esteemed the primary virtue; nor can any one become eminent among them who has not at some period of his life given proofs of his possessing this virtue. With them there can be no preferment without some warlike achievement, and so completely interwoven is this principle with the earliest elements of thought that it will, in my opinion, prove a serious obstruction to the restoration of a general peace among the nations of the Missouri.

While at Fort Mandan I was one day addressing some chiefs of the Minetares who visited us and pointing out to them the advantages of a state of peace with their neighbors over that of war in which they were engaged, the chiefs who had already gathered their harvest of laurels, and having forcibly felt in many instances some of those inconveniences attending a state of war which I pointed out, readily agreed with me in opinion.

A young fellow under the full impression of the idea I have just suggested asked me, if they were in a state of peace with all their neighbors, what the nation would do for chiefs? He added that the chiefs were now old and must shortly die, and that the nation could not exist without chiefs, taking as granted that there could be no other mode devised for making chiefs but that which custom had established through the medium of warlike achievements.

Lewis, August 24, 1805

Lewis and Clark departed what is now the western corner of the triangular Clark Canyon Reservoir and headed to the mountains.

August 24, 1805, mile 2990

At 12 o'clock we set out and passed the river below the forks, directing our route towards the cove along the track formerly mentioned. Most of the horses were heavy laden, and it appears to me that it will require at least 25 horses to convey our baggage along such roads as I expect we shall be obliged to pass in the mountains. I had now the inexpressible satisfaction to find myself once more underway with all my baggage and party.

Lewis, August 24, 1805

We proceeded on through a wide, level valley. The chief showed me the place that a number of his nation were killed about one year past. This valley continues 5 miles and then becomes narrow. The beavers have dammed up the river in many places. We proceeded up the main branch with a gradual ascent to the head, passed over a low mountain, and descended a steep descent to a beautiful stream. We passed over a second hill of very steep ascent and through a hilly country for 8 miles, and encamped on a small stream. We proceeded on over very mountainous country, across the head and hollows of springs.

Clark, August 18, 1805

August 24, 1805, mile 2992

Lewis and Clark named this valley Shoshone Cove. Now it is called Horse Valley.

Lewis Traveling with the Shoshones

Lewis had traveled ahead to find the Shoshones, and was returning to Clark and the main party with a group of the Indians.

I sent Drouillard and Shields before this morning in order to kill some meat, as neither the Indians nor ourselves had anything to eat. I informed the chief of my view in this measure, and requested that he would keep his young men with us, lest by their whooping and noise they should alarm the game and we should get nothing to eat. But so strongly were their suspicions excited by this measure that two parties of discovery immediately set out, one on each side of the valley, to watch the hunters, as I believe, to see whether the hunters had been sent to give information of their approach to an enemy that the Indians still persuaded themselves was lying in wait.

I saw that any further effort to prevent their going would only add strength to their suspicions, and therefore said no more. After the hunters had been gone about an hour we set out. We had just passed through the narrows when we saw one of the spies coming up the level plain under whip. The chief paused a little and seemed somewhat concerned. I felt a good deal so myself, and began to suspect that by some unfortunate accident that perhaps some of their enemies had straggled hither at this unlucky moment. But we were all agreeably disappointed on the arrival of the young man to learn that he had come to inform us that one of the white men had killed a deer. In an instant, they all gave their horses the whip and I was taken nearly a mile before I could learn what were the tidings. As I was without stirrups and an Indian behind me, the jostling was disagreeable. I therefore reigned up my horse and forbid the Indian to whip him, who had given him the lash at every jump for a mile, fearing he should loose a part of the feast. The fellow was so uneasy that he left me the horse, dismounted, and ran on foot at full speed, I am confident, a mile.

When they arrived where the deer was, which was in view of me, they dismounted and ran in, tumbling over each other like a parcel of famished dogs, each seizing and tearing away a part of the intestines which had been previously thrown out by Drouillard, who killed it. The scene was such when I arrived that had I not have had a pretty keen appetite myself, I am confident I should not have tasted any part of the venison. Shortly, each one had a piece of some description, and all were eating most ravenously. Some were eating the kidneys, the melt, and liver, and the blood was running from the corners of their mouths. Others were in a similar situation with the paunch and guts, but the exuding substance in this case from their lips was of a different description. One of the last who attracted my attention particularly had been fortunate in his allotment, or rather, active in the division. He had provided himself with about nine feet of the small guts, one end of which he was chewing on, while with his hands he was squeezing the contents out at the other. I really did not until now think that human nature ever presented itself in a shape so nearly allied to the brute creation. I viewed these poor starved devils with pity and compassion. I directed McNeal to skin the deer and reserved a quarter. The balance I gave the chief to be divided among his people. They devoured the whole of it nearly without cooking.

I now bore obliquely to the left in order to intercept the creek where there was some brush to make a fire, and arrived at this stream where Drouillard had killed a second deer. Here nearly the same scene was enacted. A fire being kindled, we cooked and ate, and gave the balance of the two deer to the Indians who ate the whole of them, even to the soft parts of the hoofs. Drouillard joined us at breakfast with a third deer. Of this, I reserved a quarter and gave the balance to the Indians. They all appeared now to have filled themselves and were in a good humor.

This morning early, soon after the hunters set out, a considerable part of our escort became alarmed and returned. 28 men and 3 women only continued with us. After eating and suffering the horses to graze about 2 hours, we renewed our march, and towards evening arrived at the lower part of the cove. Shields killed an antelope on the way, a part of which we took and gave the remainder to the Indians.

Lewis, August 16, 1805

August 25, 1805, mile 3008

On August 10, Lewis passed by here on his search for the Indians. On his return he passed here again on August 16.

On August 18, Clark and eleven men went ahead of the main group to determine the feasibility of descending from the mountains by river, after the Indians warned them about waterfalls, narrow canyons, lack of game, and lack of timber. Clark camped in this area on his first night out.

A week later, Lewis and the main group passed by once more with the horses and equipment.

August 25, 1805, mile 3014

The expedition ascended this valley to Lemhi Pass.

August 25, 1805, mile 3019

The Lewis and Clark Expedition crossed the Continental Divide at Lemhi Pass, elevation 7,373 feet.

August 26, 1805, mile 3028

Lemhi Pass is a National Historic Landmark in the Beaverhead Deerlodge National Forest. It is on the state border, 26 miles southeast of Salmon, Idaho and 28 miles west of Clark Canyon Reservoir, Montana.

At the distance of 4 miles further, the road took us to the most distant fountain of the waters of the mighty Missouri, in search of which we have spent so many toilsome days and restless nights. Thus far I had accomplished one of those great objects on which my mind has been unalterably fixed for many years. Judge then of the pleasure I felt in allaying my thirst with this pure and ice cold water which issues from the base of a low mountain or hill of a gentle ascent for a mile. The mountains are high on either hand, leave this gap at the head of this rivulet through which the road passes. Here I halted a few minutes and rested myself.

Two miles below, McNeal had exultingly stood with a foot on each side of this little rivulet and thanked his god that he had lived to bestride the mighty, and heretofore deemed endless, Missouri. After refreshing ourselves, we proceeded on to the top of the dividing ridge from which I discovered immense ranges of high mountains still to the west of us, with their tops partially covered with snow. I now descended the mountain about ¾ of a mile, which I found much steeper than on the opposite side, to a handsome, bold running creek of cold clear water. Here I first tasted the water of the great Columbia River.

Lewis, August 12, 1805

August 26, 1805, mile 3028

Across Idaho

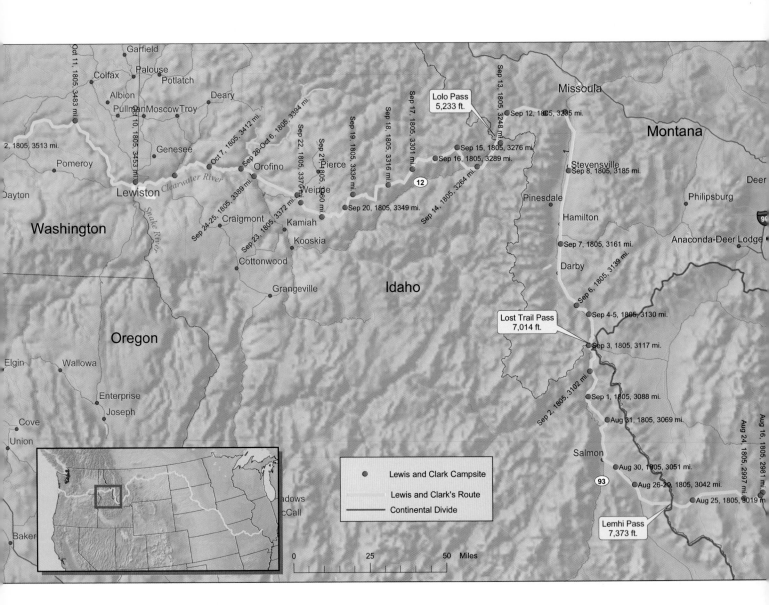

Lewis and Clark followed their Indian guide through the Rocky Mountains of Idaho on horseback until they reached the Clearwater River near Orofino. The expedition experienced some of their most difficult and uncomfortable traveling during their six weeks across Idaho.

August 26, 1805, mile 3032

Lewis and Clark crossed these hills to reach the Lemhi River Valley in the distance.

Viewed from the west, this is likely the valley that Lewis and Clark descended into the Lemhi River Valley.

August 26, 1805, mile 3038

> We set out very early on the Indian road, which still led us through an open, broken country in a westerly direction. A deep valley appeared to our left at the base of a high range of mountains which extended from the southeast to the northwest, having their sides better clad with pine timber than we had been accustomed to see in the mountains. Their tops were also partially covered with snow. At the distance of 5 miles, the road, after leading us down a long descending valley for 2 miles, brought us to a large creek about 10 yards wide. This we passed, and on rising the hill beyond it, had a view of a handsome little valley to our left of about a mile in width, through which, from the appearance of the timber, I conjectured that a river passed.
>
> *Lewis, August 13, 1805*

August 26, 1805, mile 3038

In this view downstream, the Lemhi River flows into the Salmon River at the base of the mountains in the distance. Lewis and Clark named today's Salmon River the Lewis River, and the Lemhi River they called the East Fork of Lewis's River.

The Shoshone villages were in this valley. The main group of the expedition camped here from August 26 to August 29 while Clark went about 45 miles down the Salmon River. He decided that in addition to there being no timber suitable for canoe construction, the river was impossible to descend in a canoe. It would have required descending several rapids, including the Pine Creek Rapids, a class III stretch popular with rafters and kayakers today.

The Lemhi County Airport is between the Lemhi and Salmon rivers, about 4 miles south of their confluence near Salmon, Idaho.

August 31, 1805, mile 3053

August 31, 1805, mile 3053

About 8 o'clock a.m. a number of Indians arrived here from the east side of the mountains. They belonged to this nation but had been gone a long time in the plain. One of the warriors had been scalped by some war party in the plain. A number of their relations cried aloud when they arrived in the village.

Whitehouse, August 29, 1805

August 31, 1805, mile 3053

When we crossed Lemhi Pass, an aviation chart slipped away in the wind, a hazard of an open-cockpit airplane. After we landed in Salmon, we learned that we didn't lose the chart after all. Amazingly, it got caught on a support cable and stayed there even after we landed.

Those Indians [Shoshones] are mild in their disposition, appear sincere in their friendship, and are punctual and decided. They are kind with what they have to spare. They are excessively poor, with nothing but horses. Their enemies, which are numerous on account of their horses and defenseless situation, have deprived them of tents and all the small conveniences of life.

The women are held more sacred among them than any nation we have seen, and appear to have an equal share in all conversations, which is not the case in any other nation I have seen. Their boys and girls are also permitted to speak, except in councils.

Clark, August 21, 1805

August 31, 1805, mile 3057

These cliffs border the Salmon River between Salmon and Carmen, Idaho.

One Deer was killed this morning, and a salmon in the last creek 2½ feet long. The westerly fork of the Columbia River is double the size of the easterly fork, and below those forks the river is about the size of the Jefferson River near its mouth, or 100 yards wide. It is very rapid and shoaly. The water is clear, and there is but little timber.

This cliff [probably near Tower Creek] is of a reddish brown color. The rocks which fall from it are a dark brown flint, tinged with that color. There are some gullies of white sandstone and sand fine and white as snow. The mountains on each side are high. Those on the east are rugged and contain a few scattering pine. Those on the west contain pine on their tops and high up the hollows. The bottoms of this day are wide and rich from some distance above the place I struck the east fork. They are also wide on the east.

I passed a large creek which falls in on the right side 6 miles below the forks. A road passes up this creek and to the Missouri. [This road probably goes to the Wisdom River and follows it to the Missouri. See the map on page 163.]

Clark, August 21, 1805, in advance of the main party

Wide, rich bottomland described by Clark is found at Carmen, Idaho.

August 31, 1805, mile 3059

August 31, 1805, mile 3065

Tower Creek enters the Salmon River just beyond this bend. The expedition departed the Salmon River and ascended an Indian road along Tower Creek.

The expedition turned right and departed the Salmon River just before this point on August 31. Clark had walked about 40 miles farther down the river a few days earlier to see if it would be better to follow the Salmon River out of the mountains. He found the river impossible to descend by canoe, the mountains very difficult to cross on foot, and did not find any timber in the area suitable for building canoes. The Indians had told them this beforehand, but Lewis and Clark wanted to be sure.

> We proceeded up the run [Tower Creek] on a tolerable road 4 miles and encamped in some old lodges at the place the road leaves the creek and ascends the high country. Six Indians followed us, four of them the sons of our guide. This day is warm and sultry. The prairies or open valleys are on fire in several places. The country is set on fire for the purpose of collecting the different bands, and a band of the Flat Heads, to go to the Missouri where they intend passing the winter near the buffalo. We proceeded 22 miles today, 4 miles of which was up a run.
>
> *Clark, August 31, 1805*

August 31, 1805, mile 3062

September 2, 1805, mile 3093

Lewis and Clark named the stream in this valley Fish Creek. It is now known as the North Fork of the Salmon River.

We flew along the North Fork of the Salmon River up to Lost Trail Pass, a few miles ahead.

September 2, 1805, mile 3093

The North Fork of the Salmon has steep banks and lots of undergrowth near the river. The expedition used Indian trails or "roads" on higher ground because that was the most practical way to travel with the horses. Even so, many of the horses fell on the steep slopes over the next several days.

September 2, 1805, mile 3093

A cloudy morning, it rained some last night. We set out early and proceeded on up the Fish Creek. We crossed a large fork from the right and one from the left. At 7½ miles we left the road on which we were pursuing and which leads over to the Missouri, and proceeded up a west fork of the creek without a road. We proceeded on through thickets in which we were obliged to cut a road, over rocky hillsides where our horses were in perpetual danger of slipping to their certain destruction, and up and down steep hills where several horses fell. Some turned over, and others slipped down steep hillsides. One horse was crippled and two gave out. With the greatest difficulty we made 5 miles [15 miles total for the day] and encamped on the left side of the creek in a small stony bottom. It was after night some time before the rear came up. One load was left about 2 miles back, the horse on which it was carried crippled. There was some rain at night.

Clark, September 2, 1805

September 2, 1805, mile 3094

Some of the slopes in this area are steep and impassable for horses.

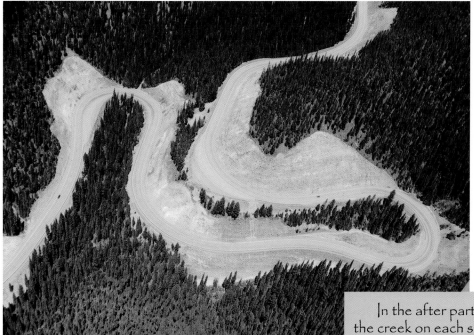

Highway 93 makes a winding ascent to Lost Trail Pass, elevation 7014 feet. Lewis and Clark lost the trail right about here.

September 3, 1805, mile 3114

In the after part of the day, the high mountains closed the creek on each side and obliged us to take on the steep sides of those mountains, so steep that the horses could scarcely keep from slipping down. Several slipped and injured themselves very much. With great difficulty we made 14 miles and encamped on a branch of the creek we ascended after crossing several steep points and one mountain.

There is but little to eat. I killed 5 pheasants and the hunters 4. With a little corn this afforded us a kind of supper. At dusk it began to snow, at 3 o'clock some rain. The mountains we passed to the east are covered with snow. We met with a great misfortune in having our last thermometer broken, by accident.

This day we passed over immense hills and some of the worst roads that ever horses passed. Our horses frequently fell. There was snow about two inches deep when it began to rain, which terminated in sleet.

Clark, September 3, 1805

Some of the mountains were so steep and rocky that several of the horses fell back among the rocks, nearly killing them. Some places we had to cut the road through thickest of balsam fir.

Whitehouse, September 3, 1805

September 4, 1805, mile 3118

The expedition spent a cold night on the mountain behind this ski area after their guide took them up the wrong creek. As a result, this pass is now called Lost Trail Pass. The next day they descended north, down the west fork of Camp Creek. Highway 93 follows Camp Creek into the East Fork of the Bitterroot River about 10 miles north of Lost Trail Pass. As they crossed the pass, they re-entered Montana but were still on the Pacific side of the Continental Divide, as shown on the map on page 180.

September 6, 1805, mile 3136

The East Fork of the Bitterroot River crosses these hills into the broad Bitterroot Valley.

Some little rain, we purchased two fine horses and took a vocabulary of the language of the Indians. We lightened our loads and packed up. Rain continued until 12 o'clock. We set out at 2 o'clock, at the same time the Indians set out on their way to meet the Snake Indians at the Three Forks of the Missouri.

We encamped in a small bottom on the right side. It rained this evening. There was nothing to eat but berries, our flour out, and but little corn. The hunters killed two pheasants only. All our horses we purchased from the Flatheads we secured well, for fear of them leaving us, and we watched them all night for fear of their leaving us, or the Indians pursuing and stealing them.

Clark, September 6, 1805

It was a very cold morning with everything wet and frozen. We were detained until 8 o'clock to thaw the covering for the baggage, etc. The ground was covered with snow. We ascended a mountain and took a dividing ridge, which we kept for several miles, and fell on the head of a creek which appeared to run the course we wished to go. I was in front and saw several of the argali or ibex [bighorn sheep].

We descended the mountain by a very steep descent, taking the advantage of the points and best places. We descended to the creek where our hunters killed a deer, which we made use of. We pursued our course down the creek to the forks, about 5 miles, where we met a party of the Tushepaw nation of 33 lodges, about 80 men, 400 total, and at least 500 horses.

Those people received us friendly, threw white robes over our shoulders, and smoked in pipes of peace. We encamped with them and found them friendly, but they had nothing but berries to eat, a part of which they gave us. Those Indians are well dressed with skin shirts and robes. They are stout and light complected more so than common for Indians. The chief harangued until late at night, smoked in our pipe, and appeared satisfied. I was the first white man who ever was on the waters of this river.

Clark, September 4, 1805

September 7, 1805, mile 3150

Darby, Montana is situated on the Bitterroot River between the "high mountains covered with snow and timber" and the prairie hills.

We proceeded on down the creek, and in our way we were met by a hunter, who had not come in last night and who had lost his horse. We halted at 12 o'clock, and one of the hunters killed two deer, which was the subject of much joy and congratulation. Here we remained to dine, and some rain fell. On the south of this place there are very high mountains covered with snow and timber, and on the north, prairie hills. After staying here two hours we proceeded on down the creek. We found the country much the same as that which we passed in the forenoon, and having traveled about 20 miles since the morning, encamped for the night. The valley has become more extensive, and our creek has increased to a considerable river. Some rain fell in the afternoon, and our hunters killed two cranes on our way.

Gass, September 7, 1805

This "high, snow-topped mountain" is on the west side of the Bitterroot Valley near Florence, Montana. The expedition descended the Bitterroot Valley to Lolo Creek, about 8 miles south of Missoula.

The morning was wet, and we proceeded on over some beautiful plains. One of our hunters had remained out all night. At noon we halted and they all came in, having killed an elk and a deer. At 2 we proceeded on again. We had a cold, wet, and disagreeable afternoon, but our road or way was level along the valley. Having traveled 20 miles, we encamped and out hunters came in. One hunter had killed a deer, and another had caught two mares and a colt, which he brought with him.

Gass, September 8, 1805

Logging roads crisscross this mountain near Florence.

We continued our journey down the river. The soil of the valley is poor and gravelly. The high snow-topped mountains are still in view on our left.

Gass, September 9, 1805

The town of Lolo is the site of Traveler's Rest, the expedition's campsite of September 9 and 10. Lolo Creek runs right-to-left across the bottom of this photo, and the Bitterroot River, at the top of the photo, goes on to Missoula to the north. On their return trip in 1806, Lewis and Clark camped here for three days before they departed on separate routes to the Missouri.

September 9, 1805, mile 3205

This evening one of our hunters returned, accompanied by three men of the Flathead nation whom he had met in his excursion up Travelers Rest Creek. On first meeting him, the Indians were alarmed and prepared for battle with their bows and arrows, but he soon relieved their fears by laying down his gun and advancing towards them. The Indians were mounted on very fine horses, of which the Flatheads have in great abundance; that is, each man in the nation possesses from 20 to 100 head.

Our guide could not speak the language of these people, but soon engaged them in conversation by signs or gesticulation, the common language of all the aborigines of North America. It is one language understood by all of them, and appears to be sufficiently copious to convey with a degree of certainty the outlines of what they wish to communicate.

In this manner we learnt from these people that two men, which they supposed to be of the Snake nation, had stolen 23 horses from them, and that they were in pursuit of the thieves. They told us they were in great haste. We gave them some boiled venison, of which they ate sparingly. The sun was now set. Two of them departed after receiving a few small articles which we gave them, and the third remained, having agreed to continue with us as a guide.

He agreed to introduce us to his relations, whom he informed us were numerous and resided in the plain below the mountains on the Columbia River, from whence, he said, the water was good and capable of being navigated to the sea. He said that some of his relations were at the sea last fall and saw an old white man who resided there by himself, and who had given them some handkerchiefs such as he saw in our possession. He said it would require five sleeps. [Instead of 5 days, it took more than 50 for the expedition to reach the ocean.]

Lewis, September 10, 1805

Our guide could not inform us where this river discharges itself into the Columbia River. He informed us that it continues its course along the mountains to the north, as far as he knew it, and that not very distant from where we then were, it formed a junction with a stream nearly as large as itself. This stream [the Hellgate] took its rise in the mountains near the Missouri to the east of us and passed through an extensive valley, generally open prairie, which forms an excellent pass to the Missouri. The point of the Missouri where the Indian pass intersects it is about 30 miles above the Gates of the Rocky Mountains, or the place where the valley of the Missouri first widens into an extensive plain after entering the Rocky Mountains. The guide informed us that a man might pass to the Missouri from hence by that route in four days.

Lewis, September 9, 1805

Lewis and Clark must have been surprised when their guide told them here that they were only four days away from the Missouri River, below the Gates of the Mountains. It had taken the expedition about 80 days to get here from the Gates of the Mountains. On the return trip the following spring, Lewis took a group of men from Traveler's Rest across the mountains on a more direct route. They made it from here to their camp above Great Falls, Montana in 10 days.

September 11, 1805, mile 3210

Lewis and Clark departed the Bitterroot River to ascend Lolo Creek to the west, toward Lolo Pass. They called this creek Traveler's Rest Creek. Their guide reported that "no game is to be found on our route for a long ways." The expedition camped in this valley on September 11.

We passed a tree on which was a number of shapes drawn on it with paint by the natives. A white bear skin hung on the same tree. We suppose this to be a place of worship among them.

Whitehouse, September 11, 1805

We proceeded on up the creek on the right side through a narrow valley and good road, and encamped at some old Indian lodges. Nothing was killed this evening. The hills on the right are high and rugged, the mountains on the left are high and covered with snow. The day is very warm.

Clark, September 11, 1805

September 12, 1805, mile 3216

We started early on your journey and had a fine morning. Having traveled 2 miles, we reached the mountains, which are very steep; but the road over them pretty good, as it is much traveled by the natives, who come across the Flathead River to gather cherries and berries. Our hunters in a short time killed 4 deer. At noon we halted at a branch of the creek, on the banks of which are a number of strawberry vines, haws, and serviceberry bushes. At 2 o'clock we proceeded on over a large mountain, where there is no water. We could find no place to encamp until late at night, when we arrived at a small branch. We encamped by it in a very inconvenient place, having come 23 miles.

Gass, September 12, 1805

Lewis and Clark continued up this valley to Lolo Pass, 30 miles ahead by their calculations.

September 13, 1805, mile 3247

Highway 12 crosses Lolo Pass at an elevation of 5,233 feet. Lewis and Clark once again moved from present-day Montana into Idaho when they crossed this pass. The main group traveled to the left of Highway 12 here on higher ground, possibly because Highway 12 had not yet been built.

When we had gone 2 miles, we came to a most beautiful warm spring, the water of which is considerably above blood heat, and I could not bear my hand in it without uneasiness. There are so many paths leading to and from this spring that our guide took a wrong one for a mile or two, and we had bad traveling across until we got into the road again. At noon we halted. Game is scarce, and our hunters killed nothing since yesterday morning, though four of the best were constantly out, and every one of them furnished with a good horse. At 2 o'clock we found a deer which our hunters had killed and hung up. We passed over a dividing ridge to the waters of another creek, up which there are some prairies or plains.

Gass, September 13, 1805

In this area, there were usually about four hunters scattered ahead of the group looking for game. Clark and some others would climb to visible points so they could keep track of their route with course and distance. Each day throughout their trip to the Pacific, they would record enough points to describe their route. Clark copied some of the descriptions in these notes into the body of his journal.

Course and Distance, September 13th, 1805

S.W.   2 miles up the said creek, through an immensely bad road, rocks, steep hillsides, and fallen timbers innumerable. The snow-topped mountains are at a long distance from the southwest to the southeast. None else to be seen in any other directions to hot springs on the right. Those springs come out of many places in the rocks and nearly boiling hot.

S. 30° W.   3 miles to the creek. We passed a round about of miles to our left of intolerable road, timber, etc. As usual, we halted to noon it. We waited for Captain Lewis who lost his horse.

S. 30° W.   7 miles over a mountain and a dividing ridge of flat, gladey land to a creek from the left passing through a glade of half a mile in width, keeping down the creek 2 miles and encamped. The country is usual except the glades, which are open and boggy. The water is clear and sandy. Snow-topped mountains to the S.E. at the head of this creek which we call the _____ Creek. The after part of the day was cloudy. I killed 4 pheasants and Shields killed a black tail deer. A horse was found in the glades left lame by some Indians.

m. 12

Clark, September 13, 1805, over Lolo Pass

Highway 12 crosses Glade Creek just before it meets Colt Killed Creek to form the Flathead River, about 4 miles east of Lolo Pass. Using today's nomenclature, the Crooked Fork meets White Sand Creek to form the Lochsa River.

In the valleys it rained and hailed, on the top of the mountains some snow fell. We crossed Glade Creek at a place the Indians have made 2 weirs across to catch salmon, and have but lately left the place. I could see no fish, and the grass has been entirely eaten out by their horses.

We proceeded on 2 miles and encamped opposite a small island at the mouth of a branch on the right side of the river, which is at this place 80 yards wide, swift, and stony. Here we were compelled to kill a colt for our men and ourselves to eat for the want of meat, and we named the south fork Colt Killed Creek. This river we call the Flat Head River. The mountains we passed today were much worse than yesterday, the last extremely bad and thickly strewn with fallen timber, pine, spruce, fir, hackmatack, and tamarack. It was steep and stony. Our men and horses are much fatigued.

Clark, September 14, 1805

September 14, 1805, mile 3262

The road leaves the river and ascends a mountain, winding in every direction to get up the steep ascents and to pass the immense quantity of fallen timber. The timber had been falling from different causes, such as fire and wind, and has deprived the greater part of the southerly sides of this mountain of its green timber.

Several horses slipped and rolled down steep hills, which hurt them very much. The one that carried my desk and small trunk turned over and rolled down a mountain for 40 yards, and lodged against a tree. It broke the desk, but the horse escaped and appeared but little hurt. Some others are very much hurt.

We proceeded on up the mountain, steep and rugged as usual. From this mountain I could observe high, rugged mountains in every direction as far as I could see. With the greatest exertion, we could only make 12 miles up this mountain. We encamped on the top of this mountain near a bank of old snow about 3 feet deep lying on the northern side of the mountain, and in small banks on the top and level parts of the mountain. We melted this snow to drink, and to cook our horse flesh to eat.

Clark, September 15, 1805

This part of the Flathead (Lochsa) River was considered impassable for horses. The expedition left the river a short distance upstream from this canyon, and followed the Indian road to the north.

September 15, 1805, mile 3268

September 16, 1805, mile 3287

These photos were taken in June, but Clark described similar amounts of snow when they passed here in September.

When we awoke this morning, to our great surprise we were covered with snow which had fallen about 2 inches in the latter part of the night, and continues a very cold snowstorm. We mended up our moccasins. Some of the men without socks wrapped rags on their feet. We loaded up our horses and set out without anything to eat, and proceeded on. We could hardly see the old trail for the snow.

Whitehouse, September 16, 1805

September 17, 1805, mile 3290

It began to snow about 3 hours before daybreak and continued all day. The snow in the morning was 4 inches deep on the old snow, and by night we found it 6 to 8 inches deep. I walked in front to keep the road, and found great difficulty in keeping it, as in many places the snow had entirely filled up the track and obliged me to hunt several minutes for the track. At 12 o'clock we halted on the top of the mountain to warm and dry ourselves a little, as well as to let our horses rest and graze a little on some long grass which I observed.

I have been wet and as cold in every part as I ever was in my life. Indeed, I was at one time fearful my feet would freeze in the thin moccasins which I wore. In the middle of the day, I took one man and proceeded on as fast as I could, about 6 miles to a small branch passing on the right. We halted and built fires for the party against their arrival, which was at dusk. Very cold and much fatigued, we encamped at this branch in a thickly timbered bottom which was scarcely large enough for us to lie level. The men were all wet, cold, and hungry. We killed a second colt, which we all supped heartily on and thought was fine meat.

Clark, September 16, 1805

September 17, 1805, mile 3290

This is probably a view of the same valley and high mountain that Clark described September 18, 1805.

September 22, 1805, mile 3367

The road was excessively bad, with snow on the knobs and no snow in the valleys. We killed a few pheasants, which were not sufficient for our supper. This compelled us to kill something. A colt, being the most useless part of our stock, fell prey to our appetites. We made only 10 miles today. Two horses fell and hurt themselves very much.

Clark, September 17, 1805

The immense mountains dampened the spirits of the party, which induced us to resort to some plan of reviving their spirits. I determined to take a party of six hunters and proceed on in advance to some level country, where there was game to kill for some meat, and send it back.

From the top of a high part of the mountain at 20 miles, I had a view of an immense plain and level country to the southwest and west. At a great distance I saw a high mountain in advance beyond the plain. We saw but little sign of deer and nothing else. There was much fallen timber. We made 32 miles and encamped on a bold running creek passing to the left, which I call Hungry Creek as at that place we had nothing to eat.

Clark, September 18, 1805

We set out early and proceeded on up the Hungry Creek, passing through a small glade at 6 miles, at which place we found a horse. I directed him killed and hung up for the party, after taking breakfast off for ourselves, which we thought fine.

Clark, September 19, 1805

At 12 miles I descended the mountain to a level pine country. I proceeded on through a beautiful country for 3 miles to a small plain in which I found many Indian lodges. I met three Indian boys. When they saw me, they ran and hid themselves in the grass. I dismounted, gave my gun and horse to one of the men, searched in the grass, and found two of the boys. I gave them small pieces of ribbon and sent them forward to the village.

Soon after, a man came out to meet me, with great caution, and conducted me to a large spacious lodge. He told me by signs that the lodge was the lodge of his great chief who had set out 3 days previous with all the warriors of the nation to war on a southwest direction, and would return in 15 or 18 days.

The few men in the village and a great number of women gathered around me with much apparent signs of fear, and apparently pleased. Those people gave us a small piece of buffalo meat, some dried salmon, berries, and roots in different states. Some of the roots which they call quamash are round like an onion and sweet. Of this they make bread and soup. They also gave us the bread made of this root, all of which we ate heartily.

We proceeded on with a chief to his village 2 miles in the same plain, where we were treated kindly in, their way, and continued with them all night.

We proceeded on, up and down several hills, and followed a ridge where the fallen timber was so thick across the trail that we could hardly get along. Our horses got stung by the yellow wasps.

Whitehouse, September 20, 1805

September 24, 1805, mile 3389

Clark spent the night with the Nez Perce Indians in this valley. He sent a horse load of provisions back to Lewis and the main group. Three days later, the main group stayed here for two nights. The end of the runway at the Orofino, Idaho airport is barely visible inside the far bend of the river.

Immense quantities of the quamash root are gathered and piled about the plain. I find myself very unwell all the evening from eating the fish and roots too freely. I sent out hunters. They killed nothing, but saw some signs of deer.

Clark, September 20, 1805

September 26, 1805, mile 3393

Dworshak Dam holds back the North Fork of the Clearwater just before it enters the Clearwater River. Lewis and Clark called the Clearwater River the Kooskooskee, and considered it the same river as the Lochsa River, the one they left 11 days earlier, to begin their difficult overland march.

The expedition spent 10 days, until October 6, at the "canoe camp" in this neighborhood, across from the mouth of the North Fork of the Clearwater. They built 5 canoes to take down the river. Most or all of the men were sick for days with gastrointestinal problems. This may have been from a drastic change in diet or contaminated food or water, complicated by their weakened condition from the hard trip over the mountains.

We had all our horses, 38 in number, collected and branded. We cut off their fore top and delivered them to the two brothers and one son of one of the chiefs who intends to accompany us down the river. To each of those men I gave a knife and some small articles. They promised to be attentive to our horses until we should return.

There was nothing to eat except dried fish and roots. Captain Lewis and myself ate a supper of roots boiled, which filled us so full of wind that we were scarcely able to breathe. All night we felt the effects of it.

We had all our saddles collected, a hole dug, and in the night buried them. Also, a canister of powder and a bag of balls were buried at the place the canoe which Shields made was cut from the body of the tree. The Saddles were buried on the side of a bend about ½ mile below. All the canoes were finished this evening and ready to be put into the water. I am taken very unwell with a pain in the bowels and stomach, which is certainly the effects of my diet. This lasted all night.

Clark, October 5, 1805

All the canoes were put into the water and loaded. We fixed our canoes as well as possible and set out. As we were about to set out, we missed both of the chiefs who promised to accompany us. I also missed my pipe tomahawk, which could not be found.

We proceeded on and passed 10 rapids which were dangerous. The canoe in which I was struck a rock and sprung a leak in the third rapid. We proceeded on 20 miles and encamped on a starboard point, opposite a run.

We had the canoes unloaded, examined, and mended a small leak which we discovered in a thin place in her side. We passed several camps of Indians today. The lodges are of sticks set in the form of the roof of a house, and covered with mats and straw.

Clark, October 7, 1805

October 7, 1805, mile 3402

Lewis and Clark passed by here on October 7, about 13 miles downstream from the Orofino airport. Highway 12 rejoined the Lewis and Clark route a few miles upstream. The Camas Prairie Railroad parallels the river opposite the highway.

October 8, 1805, mile 3413

We passed 15 rapids, four islands, and a creek on the starboard side at 16 miles. Just below the creek one canoe, in which Sergeant Gass was steering, was nearly turning over. She sprung a leak, or split open on one side, and the bottom filled with water. The canoe sunk on the rapid.

The men, several of which could not swim, hung onto the canoe. I had one of the other canoes unloaded, and with the assistance of our small canoe and one Indian canoe, we took out everything and towed the empty canoe on shore. One man, Thompson, was a little hurt. Everything was wet, particularly the greater part of our small stock of merchandise.

We had everything opened and two sentinels put over them to keep off the Indians, who are inclined to thieve, having stole several small articles. Those people appeared disposed to give us every assistance in their power during our distress.

We passed several encampments of Indians on the Islands, and those near the rapids, in which places they took the salmon. At one of those camps, we found our two chiefs who had promised to accompany us. We took them on board after the ceremony of smoking.

Clark, October 8, 1805

October 8, 1805, mile 3418

The Clearwater River winds around the small town of Myrtle, Idaho.

October 8, 1805, mile 3426

The Clearwater River continues to snake its way west. From the mountains to the Clearwater River, the expedition descended from an elevation of more than 7,000 feet to about 800 feet above sea level.

October 8, 1805, mile 3430

The Potlatch River, named Colter's Creek by Lewis and Clark, enters the Clearwater River just above Arrow Bridge.

October 8, 1805, mile 3432

October 8, 1805, mile 3432

Arrow Bridge joins Highway 12 on the left with Highway 3 on the right, about 12 miles upstream from Lewiston, Idaho. The Potlatch River enters the Clearwater in the lower left of this picture.

Sergeant Gass's canoe sank in the rapids near these islands. The expedition camped for two days to repair the canoe and dry its contents.

In examining our canoe, we found that by putting knees pinned to her sides and bottom, she could be made fit for service by the time the goods dried. We set four men to work on her, the others to collect rosin. At 1 o'clock she was finished, stronger than ever.

The Indians and our party were very merry this afternoon.

Clark, October 9, 1805

October 8, 1805, mile 3433

October 10, 1805, mile 3435

The Indians came down all the courses of this river on each side on horses to view us as we were descending.

Clark, October 10, 1805

Highway 12 crosses the Clearwater near North Lapwai, Idaho.

Our diet is extremely bad, having nothing but roots and dried fish to eat. All the party has greatly the advantage of me, in as much as they all relish the flesh of the dogs, several of which we purchased of the natives to add to our store of fish and roots.

Clark, October 10, 1805

October 10, 1805, mile 3440

We landed at the head of a very bad riffle, at which place we landed near eight lodges of Indians on the larboard side to view the riffle. After viewing this riffle, two canoes were taken over very well. The third stuck on a rock. It took us an hour to get her off, which was effected without her receiving a greater injury than a small split in her side which was repaired in a short time. We purchased fish and dogs of those people, dined, and proceeded on.

Clark, October 10, 1805

Interesting formations appear in the steep bluffs along the Clearwater River. From this viewpoint, the unpaved road above the railroad looks a little hazardous.

October 10, 1805, mile 3441

We arrived at a large southerly fork, which is the one we were on with the Shoshone nation. The country about the forks is an open plain on either side. The water of the south fork is a greenish blue, and the north is as clear as crystal. Worthy of remark is that not one stick of timber is on the river near the forks, and there are but a few trees for a great distance up the river we descended.

Clark, October 10, 1805

October 10, 1805, mile 3449

Lewiston, Idaho is at the junction of the Snake and Clearwater rivers, on the east side of the Snake. Clarkston, Washington is on the west side. In this view to the west, the Snake River is barely visible coming in from the left or south, just beyond the second bridge. The Snake River continues to the west after merging with the Clearwater.

October 10, 1805, mile 3452

In this view to the north, the Clearwater River from the right joins the Snake River in the foreground. The bridges in both the Snake and the Clearwater can be raised for tall vessels.

October 10, 1805, mile 3452

Lewis and Clark had named today's Salmon River the Lewis River weeks earlier when they were with the Shoshone. About 45 miles upstream from Lewiston, the Salmon River runs into the Snake River. Lewis and Clark considered these the same river and referred to them both as the Lewis River.

October 10, 1805, mile 3452

We made a fuel stop at Lewiston-Nez Perce County Airport. Clark was definitely accurate when he said there were open plains in this country.

The Potlatch complex in Lewiston, which employs more than 2,000 people, includes a sawmill, paper mill, co-generation power plant, and a tree nursery. Chips from the sawmill are pulped to make paper, and the waste is burned to generate 70% of the power used at the site.

October 10, 1805, mile 3447

October 10, 1805, mile 3448

October 11, 1805, mile 3454

Grain and lumber terminals are a common sight on the Snake River.

A pleasure boat speeds along the Snake River near the upper end of Lower Granite Lake. Dams along the Snake River raise today's water level above the rapids and riffles that Lewis and Clark experienced between Lewiston and the Columbia River.

October 11, 1805, mile 3457

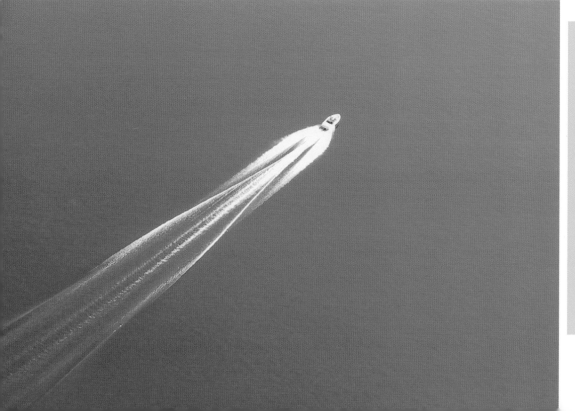

At 6 miles, we came to at some Indian lodges and took breakfast. We purchased all the fish we could and seven dogs of those people for stores of provisions down the river.

At this place I saw a curious sweat house underground, with a small hole at the top to pass in or throw in the hot stones, on which those inside threw as much water as to create the temperature of heat they wished.

Clark, October 11, 1805

Into Eastern Washington

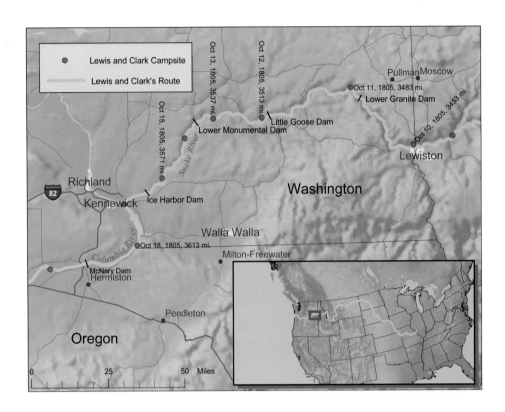

Lewis and Clark headed down the Snake River in canoes, reached the Columbia River on October 16, and continued down the Columbia toward the Pacific Ocean.

Clarkston, Washington is behind this steep bluff on the south side of the Snake River.

October 11, 1805, mile 3454

Highway 193 and the Camas Prairie Railroad hug the Lower Granite Lake shoreline. The Camas Prairie is a "short line" with less than 250 miles of railroad centered about Lewiston, Idaho.

October 11, 1805, mile 3466

At different places in the river we saw Indian houses, and slabs and split timber raised from the ground, being different parts of the houses of the natives when they reside on this river for the purpose of fishing. At this time, they are out on the plains on each side of the river hunting the antelope, as we are informed by our chiefs. Near each of those houses we observe picketed graveyards.
Clark, October 11, 1805

October 11, 1805, mile 3462

A towboat and barge move
down Lower Granite Lake
toward the Columbia.

October 11, 1805, mile 3462

October 11, 1805, mile 3462

October 11, 1805, mile 3468

Clark reported that there was no timber in this area, still true today. The Indians floated rafts of logs down the river from the forested areas above.

Although there are few trees, power lines now top the horizon.

October 11, 1805, mile 3466

A landing strip is next to the river below the Lower Granite Dam.

October 11, 1805, mile 3481

Lower Granite Dam is the uppermost of four similar dams on the lower Snake River. The Lower Granite, Little Goose, Lower Monumental, and Ice Harbor Dams were built in the 1960's and 1970's primarily for navigation and power generation. Each dam is about 100 feet high. See the map on page 204 for their locations.

October 11, 1805, mile 3480

A towboat pushes four
barges up the Snake River
through Lake Bryan.

October 12, 1805, mile 3494

October 12, 1805, mile 3494

*After purchasing every species of
provisions those Indians could spare,
we set out and proceeded on.*
                    Clark, October 12, 1805

The fields on top of the hills surrounding the
Snake River make interesting aerial scenery.

October 12, 1805, mile 3497

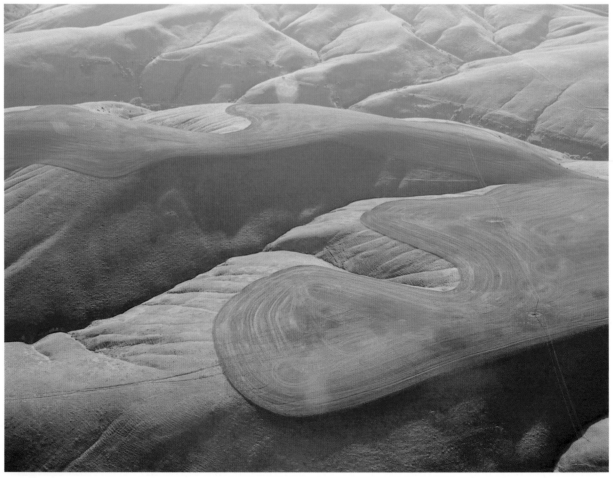

The Highway 127 Bridge spans the Snake River at Central Ferry.

October 12, 1805, mile 3498

We passed today a number of rapids, several of them very bad. We came to at the head of one at 30 miles on the starboard side, to view it before we attempted to descend through it. The Indians had told us it was very bad. We found it long and dangerous, about 2 miles in length, and many turns necessary to steer clear of the rocks which appeared to be in every direction. The Indians went through and our small canoes followed them. As it was late, we determined to camp above until morning.

Clark, October 12, 1805

October 12, 1805, mile 3509

The Little Goose Landing Strip is on the Snake River above the Little Goose Dam.

October 12, 1805, mile 3509

Here the country ascends with a gentle ascent to the high plains, and the river is 400 yards wide.

Clark, October 12, 1805

October 12, 1805, mile 3511

> We proceeded with
> two canoes at a time over
> the rapids, which are
> about 2 miles in length,
> and in about two hours we
> got all over safely.
>
> *Gass, October 13, 1805*

October 12, 1805, mile 3511

Little Goose Dam forms Lake Bryan. This lock allows boats and barges to travel through the dam. The fish ladder, to the left of the lock, allows salmon to climb over the dam to reach their spawning sites.

> We saw some ducks and
> a few geese, but did not kill
> any of them. There is no
> four-footed game of any
> kind near this part of the
> river, that we could discover,
> and we saw no birds of any
> kind but a few hawks, eagles,
> and crows.
>
> Some of the Flathead
> nation of Indians live along
> the river this far down.
> There are not more than 4
> lodges in a place or village,
> and these small camps or
> villages are 8 or 10 miles
> apart. At each camp there
> are 5 or 6 small canoes.
> Their summer lodges are
> made of willows and flags,
> and their winter lodges of
> split pine, almost like rails,
> which they bring down on
> rafts to this part of the river
> where there is no timber.
>
> *Gass, October 12, 1805*

October 12, 1805, mile 3513

This railroad "wye" is near the 2-mile long rapids that the expedition crossed on October 12 and 13. They were later called Texas Rapids, and after that were submerged in Lake Herbert G. West.

A train follows the Snake River on the south side of Lake Herbert G. West.

At 10 miles there was a little river in a starboard bend, immediately below a long, bad rapid in which the water is confined in a channel of about 20 yards between rugged rocks for the distance of a mile and a half, and a rapid, rocky channel for 2 miles above. This must be a very bad place in high water.

Clark, October 13, 1805

October 13, 1805, mile 3517

Highway 261 and the Union Pacific Railroad cross the Snake at Lyons Ferry.

October 13, 1805, mile 3523

Drouillard's River, on the right, flows into the Snake at Lyons Ferry about 50 miles northeast of Pasco, Washington. (The Snake River flows off to the left of the photo.) Drouillard's River is now called the Palouse River. The rapids that Lewis and Clark encountered here are now covered by the lake.

October 13, 1805, mile 3522

We passed a remarkable rock, very large and resembling the hull of a ship, situated on a larboard point at some distance from the ascending country.

Clark, October 14, 1805

We passed rapids at 6 and 9 miles. At 12 miles we came to at the head of a rapid which the Indians told me was very bad. We viewed the rapid and found it bad. In descending, three stern canoes stuck fast for some time on the head of the rapid, and one struck a rock in the worst part. Fortunately, all landed safe below the rapid which was nearly 3 miles in length. Here we dined, and for the first time in three weeks past I had a good dinner of blue winged teal.

After dinner we set out and had not proceeded on two miles before our stern canoe, in passing through a short rapid opposite the head of an island, ran on a smooth rock and turned broad side. The men got out on the rock, except one of our Indian chiefs who swam to shore. The canoe filled and sank. A number of articles floated out, such as the men's bedding, clothes, and skins, the lodge, etc., the greater part of which was caught by 2 of the canoes. A third canoe was unloaded and was stemming the swift current to the relief of the men on the rock, who could, with much difficulty, hold the canoe. In about an hour we got the men and canoe to shore with the loss of some bedding, tomahawks, shot pouches, skins, and clothes.

Clark, October 14, 1805

Lower Monumental Dam, viewed from downstream, is one of the four dams along the lower Snake River. It was built in 1969 and forms Lake Herbert G. West.

A train rounds a bend on Lake Sacajawea, about 20 miles northeast of Pasco, Washington.

October 15, 1805, mile 3565

We passed 11 islands and 7 rapids today. Several of the rapids were very bad and difficult to pass. The islands are of different sizes and all of round stone and sand. There is no timber of any kind in sight of the river, a few small willows excepted. In the evening the country became lower, not exceeding 90 or 100 feet above the water, and back is a wavering plain on each side. We passed through narrows for three miles where the cliffs or rocks jutted to the river on each side, compressing the water of the river through a narrow channel; below which it widens into a kind of basin, nearly round, without any perceptible current.

We examined the rapids, which we found more difficult to pass than we expected from the Indian's information. A succession of shoals appears to reach from bank to bank for 3 miles, which is also interspersed with large rocks sticking up in every direction. The channel through which we must pass is crooked and narrow.

Clark, October 15, 1805

October 15, 1805, mile 3567

We sent out hunters to hunt in the plains. About 10 o'clock they returned and informed that they could not see any signs of game of any kind.

Clark, October 15, 1805

This is an interesting point of land where Lake Sacajawea narrows. The Snake River once passed through a narrow canyon at the right of the photo, the narrows described by Clark on October 15. The narrows were flooded when the lake was formed.

October 16, 1805, mile 3582

The elevation drops that resulted in the rapids that Lewis and Clark descended are now consolidated into dams like the Ice Harbor Dam and Lock that forms Lake Sacajawea. Five Mile Rapids, where the expedition stopped and portaged ¾ mile, is about 2 miles downstream from this dam. That area is now underwater, a part of Lake Wallula.

We determined to run the rapids. We put our Indian guide in front, our small canoe next, and the other four following each other. The canoes all passed safely over except the rear canoe, which run fast on a rock at the lower part of the rapids. With the assistance of the other canoes and the Indians, who were extremely alert, everything was taken out and the canoe got off without any injury further than the articles with which it was loaded getting all wet. At 14 miles we passed a bad rapid at which place we unloaded and made a portage of ¾ mile, having passed four smaller rapids and three islands above.

Clark, October 16, 1805

We proceeded on 7 miles to the junction of this river and the Columbia, which joins from the northwest. In every direction from the junction of those rivers is one continued low plain that rises from the water gradually, except a range of high country which runs from southwest to northeast and is on the opposite side about 2 miles distant from the Columbia.

Clark, October 16, 1805

October 18, 1805, mile 3595

Lewis and Clark finally reached the Columbia River proper on October 16, 1805. This photo, looking to the northwest, shows the Snake River merging with the Columbia from the northeast. The confluence is part of Lake Wallula. The expedition camped here for two days.

October 18, 1805, mile 3595

The Highway 395 Bridge (above) is
a mile and a half upstream from the
10th Street Bridge (right).

The 10th Street Bridge and a railroad
bridge (below) cross the Columbia to
connect Pasco and Kennewick,
Washington. Clark took a canoe up the
Columbia a few miles to look around
and meet the Indians in this area.

October 18, 1805, mile 3595

October 18, 1805, mile 3595

The principal chief came down with several of
his principal men and smoked with us. Several
men and women offered dogs and fish to sell. We
purchased all the dogs we could, but the fish,
being out of season and dying in great numbers in
the river, we did not think proper to use.
    I took two men in a small canoe and ascended
the Columbia River 10 miles to an island near the
starboard shore, on which two large mat lodges of
Indians were drying salmon, as they informed me
by signs, for the purpose of food and fuel. I do
not think it at all improbable that those people
make use of dried fish as fuel. The number of
dead salmon on the shores and floating in the
river is incredible to say. At this season they have
only to collect the fish, split them open, and dry
them on their scaffolds on which they have great
numbers. How far they have to raft their timber
they make their scaffolds of I could not learn, but
there is no timber of any sort, except small willow
bushes, in sight in any direction.

Clark, October 17, 1805

The Tri-Cities Airport, about 3 miles
northeast of the Columbia River, serves
Pasco, Kennewick, and Richland,
Washington. We stopped here for the night
after following Lewis and Clark's route from
Three Forks, Montana.

October 18, 1805, mile 3610

The BNSF Railroad follows the base of the high cliffs that Lewis and Clark described. On the 18th, the expedition camped across from these cliffs at Spring Gulch Creek, south of the Walla Walla River that Clark called a "rivulet."

October 18, 1805, mile 3611

The river passes into the range of high country, at which place the rocks project into the river from the high cliffs. The country rises here about 200 feet above the water, and is bordered with black, rugged rocks.

Clark, October 19, 1805

We saw the salmon thick, jumping in the river. Some dead salmon are in the river and along the shore.

Whitehouse, October 18, 1805

Farmers grow a wide variety of crops along the Columbia River, including wheat, corn, alfalfa, potatoes and other vegetables, and orchard fruits.

We thought it necessary to lay in a store of provisions for our voyage, and the fish being out of season, we purchased 40 dogs, for which we gave articles of little value such as bells, thimbles, knitting pins, brass wire, and a few beads.

Clark, October 18, 1805

October 18, 1805, mile 3610

We passed several islands on which were Indian fishing camps. The natives all hid themselves in their flag lodges when they saw us coming. The Indians are numerous, their camps near each other along the shores. The river is pleasant, except at the rapids which are common.

Whitehouse, October 19, 1805

A barge heads down the Columbia.

October 19, 1805, mile 3619

I ascended a high cliff about 200 feet above the water, from the top of which is a level plain extending up the river and off for a great extent. At this place the country becomes low on each side of the river, and affords a prospect of the river and country below for great extent both to the right and left. From this place I discovered a high mountain of immense height covered with snow. This must be one of the mountains laid down by Vancouver, as seen from the mouth of the Columbia River. I take it to be Mount St. Helens, distance about 120 miles.

Clark, October 19, 1805

October 19, 1805, mile 3627

The hat-shaped rock at the left of this photo, seen from the Columbia River, is the one Clark used for a navigation point. It is now the focal point of Hatrock State Park, Oregon.

14 miles to a rock on the larboard side resembling a hat, just below a rapid at the lower point of an island in the middle of the river.

Clark, October 19, 1805
Course and Distance Log

Great numbers of Indians came down in canoes to view us before we set out.

Clark, October 19, 1805

October 19, 1805, mile 3632

October 19, 1805, mile 3633

A prison, a mill, and a freight terminal border the river above McNary Dam, near Umatilla, Oregon.

October 19, 1805, mile 3633

October 19, 1805, mile 3635

This fish ladder is next to the lock at McNary Dam. McNary Dam forms Lake Wallula in the Columbia and Snake Rivers above.

Interstate 82 crosses the Columbia at Umatilla. In this area, as the expedition was crossing Umatilla Rapids, Clark and three others met a large group of Indians, 350 men plus a large number of women, who were terrified of them. The Indians believed the white men of the expedition came from the clouds and were not men. They had seen a crane that Clark shot fall from a cloudy sky, and thought it was a person. Clark's demonstration of a magnifying glass to start a fire added to their apprehensions.

October 19, 1805, mile 3636

I observed a great number of lodges on the opposite side at some distance below, and several Indians on the opposite bank passing up to where Captain Lewis was with the canoes [descending the rapids]. Others I saw on a knob nearly opposite me, at which place they delayed but a short time before they returned to their lodges as fast as they could run. I was fearful that these people might not be informed of us. I determined to take the little canoe, which was with me, and proceed with the three men in it to the Lodges.

On my approach, not one person was to be seen, except three men off in the plains, and they sheared off as I approached the shore. I landed in front of five lodges which were at no great distance from each other, and saw no person. I approached one with a pipe in my hand and entered the lodge which was nearest to me.

I found 32 persons, men, women, and a few children, sitting promiscuously in the lodge, in the greatest agitation, some crying and wringing their hands, others hanging their heads. I gave my hand to them all and made signs of my friendly disposition. I offered the men my pipe to smoke and distributed a few small articles I had in my pockets. This measure pacified those distressed people very much. [Clark and the other three men then went to the other four lodges with the similar results.]

I then sat myself on a rock and made signs to the men to come and smoke with me. Not one came out until the canoes arrived with the two chiefs, one of who spoke aloud. The Indians came out and sat by me and smoked. They said we came from the clouds and were not men.

At this time, Captain Lewis came down with the canoes in which the Indians were. As soon as they saw the squaw wife of the interpreter, they pointed to her and informed those who continued yet in the same position I first found them.

The sight of this Indian Woman [Sacagawea], wife to one of our interpreters, confirmed those people of our friendly intentions, as no woman ever accompanies a war party of Indians in this quarter.

Clark, October 19, 1805

On to the Ocean...

Western Washington and Oregon

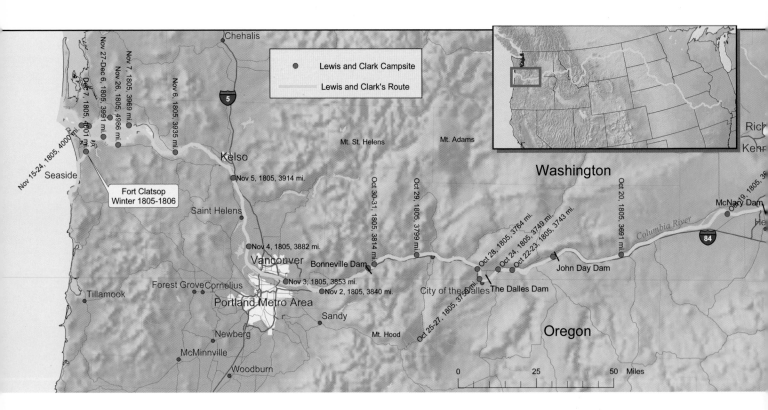

Lewis and Clark Campsite

Lewis and Clark's Route

Chehalis

Nov 7, 1805, 3969 mi.

Nov 27-Dec 6, 1805, 3991 mi.

Nov 26, 1805, 4986 mi.

Dec 7, 1805, 4001 mi.

Nov 6, 1805, 3935 mi.

Nov 15-24, 1805, 4000 mi.

Seaside

Fort Clatsop
Winter 1805-1806

Kelso

Nov 5, 1805, 3914 mi.

Saint Helens

Mt. St. Helens

Mt. Adams

Washington

Oct 30-31, 1805, 3814 mi.

Oct 29, 1805, 3799 mi.

Oct 20, 1805, 3691 mi.

Columbia River

McNary Dam

Nov 4, 1805, 3882 mi.

Vancouver

Bonneville Dam

Oct 28, 1805, 3764 mi.

Oct 24, 1805, 3749 mi.

Oct 22-23, 1805, 3743 mi.

John Day Dam

Forest Grove Cornelius

Nov 3, 1805, 3853 mi.

Nov 2, 1805, 3840 mi.

City of the Dalles

Oct 25-27, 1805, 3759 mi.

The Dalles Dam

Tillamook

Portland Metro Area

Sandy

Mt. Hood

Oregon

Newberg

McMinnville

Woodburn

0   25   50 Miles

Lewis and Clark continued down the Columbia River, across or around
several rapids, and the ocean came into view on November 7, 1805 at
the Columbia Estuary.

October 20, 1805, mile 3650

Most of this area is part of the Umatilla National Wildlife Refuge, more than 20,000 acres in size. Hundreds of thousands of ducks and geese winter in this area, and a wide variety of other birds can be found here.

October 20, 1805, mile 3655

We noticed a duck blind on the corner of this island.

October 20, 1805, mile 3655

October 20, 1805, mile 3655

We saw a number of geese, pelicans, and ducks when we flew over. Clark wrote the day the expedition passed here, "I saw a great number of pelicans on the wing, and black cormorants."

October 20, 1805, mile 3657

October 20, 1805, mile 3658

October 20, 1805, mile 3673

A railroad and a highway follow each bank of the Columbia for 175 miles from Umatilla west to Portland, Oregon. Washington Highway 14 and the BNSF Railroad, shown here, are on the north side of the river. Interstate 84 and the Union Pacific Railroad are on the Oregon side.

October 20, 1805, mile 3673

October 20, 1805, mile 3669

Power lines across the Columbia are sometimes hard to spot from the air.

October 20, 1805, mile 3661

The river today is about ¼ of a mile wide.
Clark, October 20, 1805

A barge is loaded with grain on the Columbia, west of Umatilla, Oregon.

Willow Creek flows into the Columbia from the Oregon side. On an island in this area, Clark examined an Indian burial vault, about 60 feet long and 12 feet wide. It was formed by a long ridgepole supported by two forks, 6 feet high, with pieces of canoes and boards leaning up against it. It contained numerous human remains, the most recent wrapped in leather robes. After decomposition, according to Clark, the bones were gathered in a heap and the skulls placed in a circle. The vault also contained possessions of the dead, including several horse skeletons.

October 20, 1805, mile 3676

October 20, 1805, mile 3689

After dinner we proceeded on to a bad rapid at the lower point of a small island, on which four lodges of Indians were situated, drying fish. Here the high country commences again on the starboard side, leaving a valley of 40 miles in width.

Clark, October 20, 1805

The expedition camped across from Arlington, Oregon on October 20, 1805.

A train heads up the Oregon side of the Columbia.

October 21, 1805, mile 3692

We concluded to delay until after breakfast, which we were obliged to make on the flesh of dogs. After breakfast we gave all the Indian men smoke and we set out, leaving 200 of the natives at our encampment.

Clark, October 20, 1805

October 21, 1805, mile 3700

Rocky bluffs rise above the Columbia on Interstate 84 west of Blalock, Oregon.

Last night we could not collect more dry willows, our only fuel, than was barely sufficient to cook supper, and not a sufficiency to cook breakfast this morning.

Clark, October 21, 1805

A little below is a bad rapid which is crowded with huge rocks scattered in every direction which renders the passage very difficult. A little above this rapid on the larboard side there is an immense pile of rocks. It appears as if they slipped from the cliffs under which they lay. We passed a great number of rocks in every direction scattered in the river.

Clark, October 21, 1805

The water level of the Columbia River has risen above the rocks that the expedition encountered in this area.

October 21, 1805, mile 3706

October 21, 1805, mile 3710

Interstate 84 hugs the base of a bluff, with Mount Hood barely visible 60 miles in the distance.

October 21, 1805, mile 3710

October 21, 1805, mile 3720

John Day came to this area seven years after Lewis and Clark. He was in a party of 59 people going overland to set up a Pacific Fur trading post at the mouth of the Columbia. On the way he got sick, and he and a friend were left behind with some Indians on the Snake River. The following spring, the two made it to the mouth of this river where they were attacked by hostile Indians. They lost everything they had, including their clothes. They were rescued by a group from Fort Astoria, and eventually made it to Fort Astoria at the mouth of the Columbia. After that, people began to call this river John Day's River. Of the 59 people in the Pacific Fur overland expedition, only 35 made it to the Pacific in 1811.

October 21, 1805, mile 3720

The John Day River enters the Columbia on the Washington side.

The Goldendale Aluminum smelter is above the John Day Dam on the Columbia. It was not in operation when we flew over.

October 21, 1805, mile 3721

The John Day Dam is about 25 miles up the Columbia from The Dalles. In this area Lewis and Clark met Indians with pierced noses. These Indians sometimes wore two small tapered white seashells, about 2 inches long, through the cartilage in the center of the bottom of the nose.

October 21, 1805, mile 3723

October 21, 1805, mile 3723

This part of the river is furnished with fine springs which either rise high up the sides of the hills, or on the bottom near the river, and run into the river. The hills are high and rugged. There are a few scattering trees to be seen on them, either small pine or scrubby white oak.

Clark, October 21, 1805

When we flew over this, we thought it was really odd — it looked like Stonehenge. We found out later that it *is* a replica of Stonehenge, just outside of Maryhill. It's possible that the two people in front of the motor home thought we were really odd.

This morning we saw a great number of ducks, geese, and gulls.
Gass, October 22, 1805

October 22, 1805, mile 3731

October 22, 1805, mile 3729

Mount Hood rises in the distance over the Columbia. The town of Maryhill, Washington is on the right, and Miller Island is beyond the bridge.

October 22, 1805, mile 3735

This is Miller Island, the island of rocks that Clark described on October 22, 1805. The Des Chutes River, called the Towarnahiooks by the Indians, enters the Columbia from the south, just off the left side of this picture. The Indians Lewis and Clark found in this area lived on the north side of the Columbia because their enemies lived to the south on the Des Chutes River.

October 22, 1805, mile 3737

This rock structure on Miller Island was formed by a lava flow from the north about 900,007 years ago.

These orchards are above the bluff across from the Des Chutes River.

October 22, 1805, mile 3736

We passed a bad rapid at the head of a large island in a starboard bend opposite the upper point, on which I counted 20 parcels of dried and pounded fish. Several Indians were in canoes killing fish with gigs. Opposite the center of this island of rocks, which is about 4 miles long, we discovered the entrance of a large river on the larboard side which appeared to have come from the southeast.

Clark, October 22, 1805

October 22, 1805, mile 3739

The ubiquitous railroad follows the river
beneath the high cliffs across from the
Des Chutes River.

The natives are very numerous
on the island and all along the river.
Their lodges are bulrushes and
flags, made into a kind of mats and
formed into a hut or lodge.

Gass, October 22, 1805

October 22, 1805, mile 3741

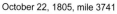

October 22, 1805, mile 3741

The BNSF Railroad tunnels through
the rocky Washington shoreline.

Interstate 84 curves into
Celilo, Oregon.

October 22, 1805, mile 3742

The railroad near Celilo forms an interesting Y-shaped intersection at the bridge across the Columbia. The expedition camped in this area at the foot of their portage around the Great Falls of the Columbia, later called Celilo Falls. The Dalles Dam has since flooded these falls. The Indians at the falls harvested tons of salmon. They preserved it so it would keep for years, and sold it to other Indians and to the white people who visited the mouth of the Columbia.

October 22, 1805, mile 3743

This portage has been frequented by the natives hauling their canoes around, and it is a great fishery with them in the spring. The fleas are now very thick, the ground covered with them. They troubled us very much this day.

Whitehouse, October 23, 1805

A section of track in the bridge can be raised for tall boats and barges.

October 22, 1805, mile 3743

Six miles below the upper mouth of the Towarnahiook River [Des Chutes] is the commencement of the pitch of the great falls. We landed and walked down, accompanied by an old man, to view the falls.

We returned, dropped down to the head of the rapids, and took every article except the canoes across the portage where I had formed a camp on an eligible situation for the protection of our stores from theft, which we were more fearful of than their arrows. Indians assisted us over the portage with our heavy articles on their horses.

Clark, October 22, 1805

I, with the greater part of the men, crossed in the canoes to the opposite side above the falls and hauled them across the portage of 457 yards, which is on the larboard side and certainly the best side to pass the canoes. At this place we were obliged to let the canoes down by strong ropes of elk skin which we had for the purpose. One canoe, in passing this place, got loose by the cords breaking and was caught by the Indians below. I accomplished this necessary business and landed sage with all the canoes at our camp below the falls by 3 o'clock p.m.

We were nearly covered with fleas. They were so thick amongst the straw and fish skins at the upper part of the portage, at which place the natives had been camped not long since, that every man of the party was obliged to strip naked during the time of taking over the canoes so that they might have an opportunity of brushing the fleas off their legs and bodies.

Great numbers of sea otters were in the river below the falls. Great numbers of Indians visit us from above and below. One of the old chiefs who had accompanied us from the head of the river informed us that he heard the Indians say that the nation below intended to kill us. We examined all the arms and completed the ammunition to 100 rounds. The natives left us earlier this evening than usual, which gives a shadow of confirmation to the information of our old chief.

I observed on the beach near the Indian lodges two beautiful canoes of different shape and size to what we had seen above. They are wide in the middle, and tapering to each end. On the bow, curious figures were cut into the wood. Captain Lewis went up to the lodges to see those canoes and exchanged our smallest canoe for one of them by giving a hatchet and a few trinkets to the owner, who informed us he purchased it of a white man below for a horse. These canoes are neater made than any I have ever seen. They are calculated to ride the waves and carry immense burthens.

Clark, October 22, 1805

Gravel is loaded from this quarry near Wishram, Washington directly into barges. The sea otters that Clark saw here were harbor seals —sea otters stay in salt water. Clark corrected this mistake later in his journals. In today's Columbia River seals do not normally live above the Bonneville Dam, the lowest dam in the river, more than 50 miles downstream from here.

To put the size of this barge into perspective, compare it to the two people in the rowboat behind the barge. To the right of the rowboat, gravel is fed through a tunnel underneath the railroad tracks.

October 24, 1805, mile 3746

Coming into The Dalles, Oregon, the Columbia once featured two major narrows, the Short Narrows of the Columbia and the Long Narrows. During the spring floods, the narrows restricted the water flow so much that the water level below Celilo Falls was temporarily raised almost as high as the top of the falls, 35 to 40 feet. In 1957 The Dalles Dam permanently raised the water level above the narrows and rapids.

The whole of this river must at all stages pass through this narrow channel of 45 yards width. As the portage of our canoes of this high rock would be impossible with our strength, I determined to pass through this place notwithstanding the horrid appearance of this agitated gut swelling, boiling, and whirling in every direction, which, from the top of the rock, did not appear as bad as when I was in it. However, we passed safely, to the astonishment of all the Indians of the last lodges who viewed us from the top of the rock.

Clark, October 24, 1805

The natives of this village received me very kindly, one of whom invited me into his house, which I found to be large and commodious. These were the first wooden houses in which Indians have lived since we left those in the vicinity of Illinois. They are scattered promiscuously on an elevated situation near a mound of about 30 feet above the common level, which mound has some remains of houses and has every appearance of being artificial.

Clark, October 24, 1805

There have been white people trading among these savages. We saw one half white child among them. We saw also a new copper tea kettle, beads, copper, and a number of other articles which must have come from some white trader.

Whitehouse, October 24, 1805

October 24, 1805, mile 3749

The city of The Dalles, Oregon, home of Meredith Van Valkenburgh, is 29 miles northeast of Mount Hood.

I saw several large scaffolds on which the Indians dry fish. As this is out of season, the poles on which they dry those fish are tied up very securely in large bundles and put upon these scaffolds. I counted 107 stacks of dried pounded fish in different places on those rocks, which must have contained 10,000 lbs. of neat fish. I returned through a rocky open country infested with polecats.

Clark, October 24, 1805

The Dalles Dam is an oddly shaped dam with a 90-degree corner. In this view upstream, the expedition followed the river to the right of the dam and back to the left just below the dam. The narrows were just upstream from the dam. The expedition almost lost a canoe when they descended the rapids that were to the right of the dam.

October 25, 1805, mile 3753

Several of the Indians stayed with us this night, one of them a chief. Captain Lewis compared the languages of these with those he had taken down all the way this side of the mountains, and finds them to be all one nation. They differ a little in their languages, caused by the different tribes of them scattered such a long distance from each other. We think the Flathead nation to be 10,000 strong in all.

Whitehouse, October 26, 1805

October 25, 1805, mile 3753

Highway 197 crosses the Columbia below The Dalles Dam.

Captain Lewis and myself walked down to see the place the Indians pointed out as the worst place in passing through the gut, which we found difficult of passing without great danger, but as the portage was impracticable with our large canoes, we concluded to make a portage of our most valuable articles and run the canoes through accordingly.

A great number of Indians were viewing us from the high rocks under which we had to pass. The first three canoes passed through very well. The fourth nearly filled with water, and the last pass through by taking in a little water. Thus safely below what I conceived to be the worst part of this channel, I felt myself extremely gratified and pleased. We loaded the canoes and set out, and had not proceeded more than two miles before the unfortunate canoe which filled crossing the bad place above ran against a rock and was in great danger of being lost.

This channel is through a hard, rough, black rock, from 50 to 100 yards wide, swelling and boiling in a most tremendous manner. Several places here the Indians inform me they take the salmon as fast as they wish.

The pinnacle of the round topped mountain which we saw a short distance below the forks of this river is at this time topped with snow. We called this the Falls Mountain or Timm Mountain. [This is Mount Hood.]

Clark, October 25, 1805

Boats, trains, automobiles, and airplanes travel today's Columbia. The railroad cuts through rock (lower left) next to the boat channel into The Dalles lock. This picture was taken on approach to The Dalles Airport.

We went about 4 miles and halted at a small village of the natives and got some dogs from them. Here we stayed about an hour and proceeded on again for about a mile, when we were compelled to stop on account of the wind, which blew so hard ahead that we were unable to continue our voyage.

Gass, October 28, 1805

October 25, 1805, mile 3753

October 25, 1805, mile 3754

We saw great numbers of white cranes flying in different directions very high.

*Clark, October 26, 1805,
observing the whooping crane.*

The Dalles Airport was windy and gusty both times we landed there. Lewis and Clark also experienced a stiff wind from the Columbia Gorge. Today, that wind makes the Columbia Gorge one of the country's top windsurfing locales. When we flew down the Columbia Gorge we intended to descend and photograph some wind surfers, but it was too windy for us.

October 29, 1805, mile 3789

This towboat heads up the Columbia Gorge into the wind. During the day there is frequently a strong wind that blows from the west through the gorge between Portland and The Dalles. When we flew along that route, we found a strong wind from the west low in the gorge, a strong wind from the east at about 4,000 or 5,000 feet altitude, and a lot of turbulence in between the conflicting air currents.

In this view upstream, the upper end of the Columbia River Gorge flattens out into broad plains.

October 29, 1805, mile 3771

October 29, 1805, mile 3771

The country on each side begins to be thicker timbered with pine and low white oak, very rocky and broken. We passed three large rocks in the river. The middle rock is large, long, and has several square [burial] vaults on it. We call this rocky island the Sepulcher.

Clark, October 29, 1805

A railroad tunnels through the rocky banks of the Columbia east of Lyle, Washington.

October 29, 1805, mile 3776

In this view to the east, a tilted geological structure slopes into the river. In the distance is Sepulcher Island, now called Mamaloose Island.

The SDS Lumber Mill has been a fixture on the Columbia at Bingen, Washington for more than 50 years.

October 29, 1805, mile 3786

October 29, 1805, mile 3792

In the evening we discovered a high mountain to the south, not more than 5 miles off, covered with snow. Here we have still water, and the breadth of the river is from three quarters of a mile to one mile.

Gass, October 29, 1805

Mount Hood is 25 miles away from the town of Hood River. Gass estimated 5 miles.

A rocky island in the Columbia.

The mountains are high on each side, containing scattering pine, white oak, and undergrowth. The hillsides are steep and rocky.

Clark, October 29, 1805

October 30, 1805, mile 3800

We passed several places where the rocks projected into the river and have the appearance of having separated from the mountains and fallen promiscuously into the river. Small niches are formed in the banks below those projecting rocks.

Clark, October 30, 1805

This day we saw some of the large buzzard. Captain Lewis shot at one. Those buzzards are much larger than any other of their species or the largest eagle. They are white under part of their wings.

Clark, October 30, 1805
describing the California condor.

October 30, 1805, mile 3810

Kayakers (in the lower left of the photo) paddle the rugged shoreline of the Columbia near Carson, Washington.

A train rounds the bend near Bridge of the Gods at Cascade Locks, Oregon, about 3 miles above Bonneville Dam. This view is upstream, to the east.

The 1,800-foot runway of Cascade Locks State Airport is just upstream from the Bridge of the Gods.

November 1, 1805, mile 3816

October 30, 1805, mile 3813

Bonneville Dam, built in 1937, is the lowest of the four dams on that part of the Columbia River descended by Lewis and Clark. The water is only 70-77 feet above sea level upstream of the dam, and 7-40 feet above sea level below the dam. The Willamette Locks, on the far side of the river in this picture, began operation in 1873. Commercial traffic through the locks has recently dropped to almost nothing, leaving the locks to recreational boat traffic. The rapids here were the last that Lewis and Clark encountered on their way to the Pacific.

November 1, 1805, mile 3821

This evening we came to the head of the falls, where there is a large Indian village. On our way we saw a great many swans, geese, and ducks, and a number of sea otters.

Gass, October 30, 1805

I could not see any rapids below, in the extent of my view which was for a long distance down the river. The last rapids widened and had every appearance of being affected by the tide.

Clark, October 31, 1805

We took down two canoes, one at a time, over high rocks on rollers, by main strength and by being in the water which ran between large rocks. We had to haul them that way past two of the worst rapids. Then we took them half a mile below, where we intend loading. This will make the portage, in all, only about 1 mile.

Whitehouse, October 31, 1805

November 1, 1805, mile 3821

We carried all our baggage past the portage. We drew out one of the canoes to repair it, then went at taking the other two large canoes and the small one. Towards evening we got it all safely below the big rapids and camped. Three canoes arrived at the head of the rapids, a number of men and women on board. They were loaded with pounded fish and dried salmon for trade. They signed to us that they are going down to the white traders to trade their fish for blue beads.

Whitehouse, November 1, 1805

Big sections of Table Mountain (left) and nearby Greenleaf Peak slid down into the Columbia River a few hundred years ago, probably in three major slides. This dammed the river temporarily, shifted its course to the south, and created the rapids that Lewis and Clark portaged. This natural dam was called the Bridge of the Gods in Indian legends, the name given to today's bridge above Bonneville Dam.

November 2, 1805, mile 3822

This 3D satellite image shows how the slide from Table Mountain altered the flow of the Columbia River in the Bonneville Dam area.

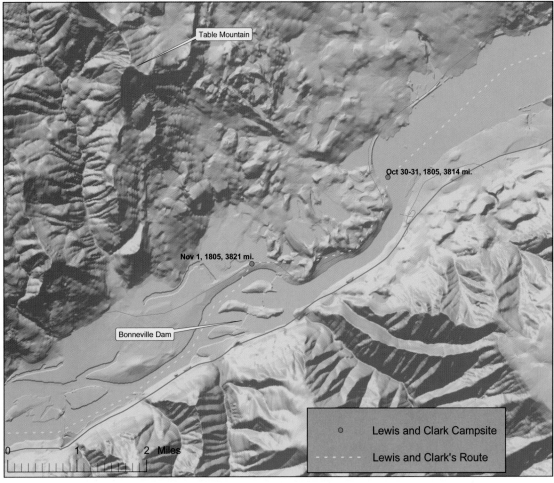

Table Mountain

Oct 30-31, 1805, 3814 mi.

Nov 1, 1805, 3821 mi.

Bonneville Dam

	Lewis and Clark Campsite
	Lewis and Clark's Route

0   1   2 Miles

Bonneville Dam and Table Mountain

Beacon Rock is the core of an ancient volcano. Clark estimated the rock at 800 feet, and he was only 40 feet off — the rock is 840 feet high. Henry Biddle purchased the rock in 1915 and completed the 1.6 mile trail to the top in 1918. His children donated Beacon Rock to the State of Washington in 1935. Nicholas Biddle, who edited the first (1814) edition of the Lewis and Clark Journals, is an ancestor of Henry Biddle.

The ebb tide rose here about 9 inches, the flood tide must rise here much higher. We saw great numbers of waterfowl of different kinds, such as swan, geese, white and gray brants [snow geese], ducks of various kinds, gulls, and plover. Labiche killed 14 brant, Joseph Fields 3, and Collins 1.

Clark, November 2, 1805

November 2, 1805, mile 3826

November 2, 1805, mile 3832

A remarkable high rock is on the starboard side, about 800 feet high and 400 yards around, the Beacon Rock.

Clark, November 2, 1805

The hills on both sides are very high. A number of fine springs flow out of them, some of which fall 200 feet perpendicularly. The hills are mostly solid rock.

Gass, November 2, 1805

The 611-foot Multnomah Falls are near Interstate 84 about 20 miles east of Portland. Latourell, Coopey, Wahkeena, and Horsetail Falls, ranging from 140 to 250 feet in height, are also in this area.

November 2, 1805, mile 3832

Reed Island is upstream from the quicksand the expedition found at the mouth of Sandy River. In 1792, George Vancouver sent Lieutenant Broughton up the Columbia in a longboat. He got as far as Reed Island, and named Mount Hood after a British admiral. The flat area in the distance is near the mouth of the Sandy River.

The fog continued so thick that we could scarcely see the shores or islands. We passed several islands. About noon we halted to dine at the mouth of a river which came in on the larboard side. The mouth was filled with quick sand so that we could run a pole 6 or 8 feet into it. The river emptied in at several places through a very large sandbar which lay at the mouth.

Whitehouse, November 3, 1805
at the mouth of Sandy River

The Fern Prairie Modelers flying field for radio controlled airplanes is near Washougal, Washington on the north shore of the Columbia.

A well-used ship is moored across from Government Island.

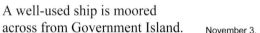

This helicopter was flying low over Government Island, near Portland, when we passed by. Lewis and Clark camped on this island on November 3, 1805.

November 3, 1805, mile 3848

November 3, 1805, mile 3848

November 3, 1805, mile 3851

November 3, 1805, mile 3846

November 3, 1805, mile 3850

November 3, 1805, mile 3846

We found a wide range of industry along the Columbia River as we approached Vancouver, Washington.

November 4, 1805, mile 3856

As we neared Portland we passed the brig *Lady Washington,* also headed down the Columbia. It is a replica of the *Lady Washington* that sailed from about 1750 to 1798. This *Lady Washington* was launched in 1989, and is featured in the 2003 movie *Pirates of the Caribbean.*

Vessels similar to this one traded with the Indians at the mouth of the Columbia. Some of the Indians made reference to a trader named Haley. Haley may have been Captain Samuel Hill of the brig *Lydia,* who had traded with the Indians of the Columbia in April 1805. He returned the following spring, after Lewis and Clark had departed on their return trip.

Towards evening we met several Indians in a canoe who were going up the river. They signed to us that in two sleeps we should see ocean vessels and white people, etc.
Whitehouse, November 3, 1805

Here we met 15 men in two canoes from below. They informed us they saw three vessels below.
Clark, November 3, 1805

Sailboats dot the Columbia next to Portland International Airport. The airport is probably the site of the large village that the expedition visited on November 4, 1805.

November 4, 1805, mile 3857

November 4, 1805, mile 3857

On the main larboard shore a short distance below the last island, we landed at a village of 25 houses. This village contains about 200 men of the Skilloot nation. I counted 52 canoes on the bank in front of this village, many of them very large and raised in the bow.

Clark, November 4, 1805

We followed this airliner on final approach into Portland International.

November 4, 1805, mile 3873

The red Broadway Bridge and the Steel Bridge cross the Willamette River on either side of Rose Garden Arena, in downtown Portland. At the time of the expedition, Hayden Island (which was three islands at the time) obscured the view of the mouth of the Willamette from the main river channel. When the expedition was outbound to the Pacific, they missed seeing the river, even though they heard about it from the Indians. On the return trip in the spring of 1806 they missed it again, but Clark backtracked with a few men and explored 10 miles up the Willamette.

November 4, 1805, mile 3873

The Steel Bridge, which spanned the Willamette in 1912, has a section that can be raised vertically. Each of the two decks can be raised independently.

November 4, 1805, mile 3873

The Broadway Bridge, built in 1913 across the Willamette, is a drawbridge. Its center section splits, and each half raises to an angle of 89 degrees.

November 4, 1805, mile 3873

The Fremont Bridge, the newest Willamette bridge in Portland, was completed in 1973.

November 4, 1805, mile 3867

A busy riverfront at Vancouver, Washington

November 4, 1805, mile 3867

Interstate 5 crosses the Columbia between Portland and Vancouver. A section of the bridge can be raised for tall vessels.

This BNSF Railroad Bridge, built in 1908, is closing after swinging open for the barge in the picture above.

November 4, 1805, mile 3866

November 4, 1805, mile 3875

November 4, 1805, mile 3870

Towards the evening we met a large canoe loaded with Indians. One of them could curse some words in English. They had a sturgeon on board. Their canoe had images worked on the bow and stern. They have five muskets on board.

Whitehouse, November 4, 1805

November 4, 1805, mile 3870

We saw several freighters that come to port at Portland and Vancouver.

November 4, 1805, mile 3869

November 4, 1805, mile 3869

When Lewis and Clark were in the lower Columbia, Indians would sometimes come for hundreds of miles to trade in this area. The major product here was dried salmon, although the local Indians also traded horses, beads, and what modern goods they could get from the trading ships at the mouth of the Columbia. This area has continued to be a center of trade ever since. Today, Subaru imports its automobiles into the U.S. through this terminal at the Port of Vancouver, USA.

We proceeded on until one hour after dark, with a view to get clear of the natives who were constantly about us and troublesome. Finding that we could not get shut of those people for one night, we landed and encamped on the starboard side. Soon after, two canoes came to us, loaded with Indians. We purchased a few roots of them. The river here is 1 ½ miles wide, the current gentle.

Clark, November 4, 1805

It rained all the after part of last night, and the rain continues this morning. I slept but very little last night for the noise kept during the whole of the night by the swans, geese, white and gray brant, ducks, etc., on a small sand island close under the larboard side. They were immensely numerous, and the noise horrid.

Clark, November 5, 1805

The Lewis River flows into the Columbia about 20 miles south of Kelso, Washington.

November 5, 1805, mile 3894

This 499-foot cooling tower is across the river from the expedition's November 5 campsite. In 1992, the Trojan Nuclear Power Plant near Goble, Oregon had some trouble with tube leaks in one of its steam generators. Facing public pressure and an estimated $200 million repair bill, Portland General Electric decided to close the plant permanently in 1993. Six years later, the 1,000-ton nuclear reactor was moved by barge up the Columbia River to the Port of Benton, about 20 miles above the Snake River. From there it was taken 30 miles by road to Hanford, Washington, where it was buried whole. The trip up the river on a specially made barge took 36 hours. It took Lewis and Clark 18 days to get here from the Snake River.

November 5, 1805, mile 3914

November 5, 1805, mile 3907

Lumber is big business along the lower Columbia, in contrast to eastern Oregon and Washington where Lewis and Clark could barely scrape up enough wood for cooking.

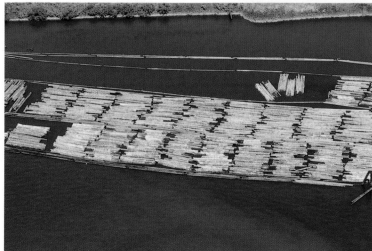

November 5, 1805, mile 3907

November 5, 1805, mile 3898

November 5, 1805, mile 3905

November 5, 1805, mile 3905

November 5, 1805, mile 3905

We flew by the United Harvest terminal in Kalama, Washington as the *Bright Coral* was being loaded.

November 5, 1805, mile 3906

This is certainly a fertile and a handsome valley, at this time crowded with Indians. The day proved cloudy with rain the greater part of it. We are all wet, cold, and disagreeable. In my walk today I saw 17 striped snakes. I killed a grouse, which was very fat and larger than common. This is the first night we have been entirely clear of Indians since our arrival on the waters of the Columbia River. We made 32 miles today by my estimation.

Clark, November 5, 1805

This cargo ship dwarfs the sailboat in the distance.

The Kalama Export Company exports corn, milo, soybeans, and wheat from its terminal on the Columbia.

November 5, 1805, mile 3913

November 6, 1805, mile 3919

The runway at the Kelso-Longview Airport (right) is next to the Cowlitz River, which flows into the Columbia near Longview, Washington. The train below was passing by as we made our approach to land.

November 6, 1805, mile 3919

The Lewis and Clark Bridge crosses the Columbia at Longview, Washington.

November 6, 1805, mile 3920

The 581-foot ship *Ace Century* is being loaded with lumber, probably destined for Japan.

November 6, 1805, mile 3921

November 6, 1805, mile 3920

The *Ace Dragon* heads out to sea, full of logs. These ships carry logs, grain, ore, and other bulk cargo.

November 6, 1805, mile 3935

There was no place for several miles sufficiently large and level for our camp. We at length landed at a place which, by moving the stones, we made a place sufficiently large for the party to lie level on the smaller stones clear of the tide.

It was cloudy with rain all day. We are all wet and disagreeable. We had large fires made on the stone and dried out our bedding and killed the fleas which collected in our blankets at every old village we encamped near.

Clark, November 6, 1805

November 6, 1805, mile 3935

November 6, 1805, mile 3934

November 6, 1805, mile 3934

The *Asian Phoenix* rides high in the water as she heads up the Columbia to take on cargo. On November 6, the expedition camped on the far shore in the top picture, near Waterford, Washington.

This bridge, built in 1939, connects Cathlamet, Washington to Puget Island. The Puget Island Ferry continues from Puget Island across to Oregon.

November 7, 1805, mile 3944

November 7, 1805, mile 3950

Ocean-going barges are usually pulled instead of being pushed.

Great joy in camp, we are in view of the Ocean, this great Pacific Ocean, which we have been so long anxious to see.

Clark, November 7, 1805

November 10, 1805, mile 3987

U.S. Highway 101 crosses the Columbia River on the 4-mile long Astoria-Megler Bridge. The expedition spent November 10 to 14 under difficult conditions a few hundred yards northeast of the far end of this bridge. It was cold and wet. The only place they could find to sleep the first night was on some drift logs, which floated up in the water during high tide.

We proceeded on about 10 miles. We saw great numbers of sea gulls. The wind rose from the northwest and the waves became so high that we were compelled to return about 2 miles to a place we could unload our canoes. We unloaded them in a small niche at the mouth of a small run on a pile of drift logs, where we continued until low water.

When the river appeared calm we loaded and set out, but were obliged to return, finding the waves too high for our canoes to ride. We again unloaded the canoes, stowed the loading on a rock above the tide water, and formed a camp on the drift logs which appeared to be the only situation we could find to lie, the hills being either a perpendicular cliff or a steep ascent, rising to about 500 feet. Our canoes we secured as well as we could. We were all wet, the rain having continued all day, also our bedding and many other articles. We employed ourselves drying our blankets.

Clark, November 10, 1805

We purchased of the Indians 13 red char, which we found to be an excellent fish. Those people left us and crossed the river (which is about 5 miles wide at this place) through the highest waves I ever saw a small vessel ride. Those Indians are certainly the best canoe navigators I ever saw. It rained all day.

Clark, November 11, 1805

It would be distressing to a feeling person to see our situation at this time, all wet and cold with our bedding also wet, in a wet bottom scarcely large enough to contain us. Our baggage is half a mile from us and the canoes are at the mercy of the waves, although secured as well as possible. We sunk them with immense parcels of stone to weight them down, to prevent their dashing to pieces against the rocks. Rain continued.

Clark, November 12, 1805

Cape Disappointment was named by John Mears in 1788 because he couldn't find the Columbia River. The Cape Disappointment lighthouse was first lit in 1856, 50 years after Lewis and Clark departed for home. The Lewis and Clark Interpretive Center is to the left of the lighthouse. The Indians came from miles around to trade here with the white people's trading ships. Lewis and Clark hoped to meet a ship at the mouth of the Columbia and replenish their supplies, but they never did see one.

Built in 1898, the North Head lighthouse is just around the corner from Cape Disappointment, about a mile to the northwest.

Clark took some members of the expedition who wanted to see the ocean on a trip up Long Beach.

After taking a sumptuous breakfast of venison, which was roasted on sticks exposed to the fire, I proceeded on through rugged country of high hills and steep hollows on a course from the cape N 20° W for five miles, on a direct line to the commencement of a sandy coast which extends N 10° W from the top of the hill above the sand shore to a point of high land distant near 20 miles.

I proceeded on this sandy coast 4 miles, and marked my name on a small pine, the day of the month, and year.

Clark, November 19, 1805

Here we made a fire and dined on 4 brant and 48 plover which were killed by Labiche on the coast as we came on. Rueben Fields killed a buzzard of the large kind near the meat of the whale we saw. It weighed 25 lbs., measured from the tips of the wings across 9 ½ feet, and from the point of the bill to the end of the tail 3 feet 10 ¼ inches.

Clark, November 18, 1805
describing a California condor
near Ilwaco, Washington

We found hundreds of seagulls, pelicans, and other birds when we flew up the beach.

In this view of the Astoria, Oregon Airport, Young's Bay is in the foreground and the Pacific Ocean is in the background to the west. Lewis and Clark crossed the Columbia Estuary, about 5 miles wide, on November 26. On December 7, they moved to the site of their winter home, Fort Clatsop, and began construction shortly afterward. The precise location of Fort Clatsop isn't known, but it is probably a mile or two south of the airport.

The sea, which is immediately in front, roars like a repeated rolling thunder and has roared in that way ever since our arrival in its borders. It is now 24 days since we arrived in sight of the Great Western Ocean; I can't say Pacific as since I have seen it, it has been the reverse.

Clark, December 1, 1805

Those people were somewhat astonished at three shots I made with my little rifle today.

After amusing myself for about an hour on the edge of the raging seas, I returned to the houses. One of the Indians pointed to a flock of brant sitting in the creek a short distance below and requested me to shoot one. I walked down with my small rifle and killed two at about 40 yards distance. On my return to the houses, two small ducks set at about 30 steps from me. The Indians pointed at the ducks. They were near together. I shot at the ducks and accidentally shot the head of one off. This duck and brant were carried to the house and every man came around, examined the duck, and looked at the gun. The size of the ball was 100 to the pound. [about .36 caliber] They said in their own language *clouch* musket, *wake, com ma-tax* musket, which is good musket, do not understand this kind of musket, etc.

Clark, December 10, 1805

A smooth beach runs almost 20 miles from the mouth of the Columbia south to Tillamook Head. The expedition set up a camp on this beach for salt extraction.

A long breakwater is on the south side of the Columbia Estuary.

Seals and sea lions use the breakwater for a resting spot.

Several Indians and squaws came this evening I believe for the purpose of gratifying the passions of our men. Those people appear to view sensuality as a necessary evil, and do not appear to abhor this as crime in the unmarried females. The young women sport openly with our men, and appear to receive the approbation of their friends and relations for so doing. Many of the women are handsome.

Clark, November 21, 1805

A sharp rock stands at the point of Tillamook Head. Clark sighted Tillamook Head from Cape Disappointment, 24 miles to the north across the Columbia Estuary. He climbed Tillamook Head a few weeks later, on his way to see a beached whale. By the time they got to the whale there was only a 105-foot skeleton. The Indians had already taken the meat, blubber, skin, and oil.

We proceeded on the round, slippery stones under a high hill which projected into the ocean about 4 miles further on the coast. After walking for 2 ½ miles on the stones, my guide made a sudden halt, pointed to the top of the mountain, and uttered the word *pe shack*, which means bad, and made signs that we could not proceed any further on the rocks but must pass over that mountain.

I hesitated a moment and viewed this immense mountain, the top of which was obscured in the clouds, and the ascent appeared to be almost perpendicular. As the small Indian path along which they had brought immense loads but a few hours before led up this mountain and appeared to ascend in a sidelong direction, I thought more than probable that the ascent might be tolerably easy and therefore proceeded on.

I soon found it became much worse as I ascended, and at one place we were obliged to support and draw ourselves up by the bushes and roots for nearly 100 feet. After about two hours of labor and fatigue, we reached the top of this high mountain, from which I looked down with astonishment to behold the height which we had ascended. It appeared to be 10 or 12 hundred feet up a mountain which appeared to be almost perpendicular.

Clark, January 7, 1805

Viewing the ocean from Tillamook Head on January 8, 1806, Clark wrote of "innumerable rocks of immense size."

We set out early and proceeded to the top of the mountain, next to which is much the highest part and that part facing the sea is open. From this point I beheld the grandest and most pleasing prospects which my eyes ever surveyed. In my front, a boundless ocean. To the north and northeast, the coast as far as my eyes could be extended, the seas raging with immense wave and breaking with great force from the rocks of Cape Disappointment as far as I could see to the northwest.

The Clatsops, Chinooks, and other villagers were on each side of the Columbia River, and in the prairies below me, the meanderings of three handsome streams heading in small lakes at the foot of the high country. I saw the Columbia River for some distance up, with its bays and small rivers.

On the other side I had a view of the coast for an immense distance to the southeast by south. The niches and points of high land which form this course for a long way, added to the innumerable rocks of immense size, out a great distance from the shore and against which the seas break with great force, give this coast a most romantic appearance.

Clark, January 8, 1806
from Tillamook Head

We found some mountaintops obscured by clouds just as Clark did.

The Tillamook Rock Lighthouse, off the coast of Tillamook Head, Oregon, was in operation from 1880 to 1957. Today the lighthouse serves as a popular roost for seabirds.

The most remarkable trait [of the Indians] is the peculiar flatness and width of forehead, which they artificially obtain by compressing the head between two boards while in a state of infancy, and from which it never afterwards perfectly recovers. This is a custom among all nations we have met with west of the Rocky Mountains. I have observed the heads of many infants after this singular bandage had been dismissed, about the age of 10 or 11 months, that were not more than two inches thick about the upper edge of the forehead, and rather thinner still higher. From the top of the head to the extremity of the nose is one straight line. This is done in order to give a greater width to the forehead, which they much admire. The process seems to be continued longer with their female than their male children, and neither appear to suffer any pain from the operation.

Lewis, March 19, 1806

The 235-foot Haystack Rock is a local landmark at Cannon Beach, Oregon.

Thousands of birds use the offshore rocks around Tillamook Head and Cannon Beach.

The coast in the neighborhood of this old village is slipping from the sides of the high hills, in immense masses. 50 or 100 acres at a time give way, and a great proportion in an instant precipitate into the ocean. Those hills and mountains are principally composed of a yellow clay. Their slipping off or splitting asunder at this time is no doubt caused by the incessant rain which has fallen within the last two months.

Clark, January 8, 1805
north of Cannon Beach, Oregon.

Success

After a cold, wet winter at Fort Clatsop near Astoria, Oregon, the expedition began their return trip. The winter at Fort Clatsop was much less enjoyable than the previous winter at Fort Mandan. The Indians were often "thievish," and it rained more days than not.

Lewis and Clark departed for home on March 23, 1806. They planned to travel inland and wait for some snow to melt before they crossed the mountains. They waited for a while, but not long enough.

On their first attempt into the mountains, they left much of their baggage and equipment in trees in the mountains, and backtracked to lower ground. After waiting some more and hiring an Indian guide, they made excellent time across the mountains to Traveler's Rest at today's Lolo, Montana, south of Missoula.

At Traveler's Rest, the expedition divided. On July 3, Lewis took a group of nine men across the mountains directly to the Great Falls of the Missouri. From there he went north to explore the Marias River. Most of their horses were lost or stolen, so Lewis took only two men with him up the Marias River. There, two of a group of Blackfeet Indians were killed trying to steal guns and horses from Lewis's group. Lewis then left Blackfeet territory as fast as he could. He caught up with Clark a few days later on the Missouri, downstream from the mouth of the Yellowstone.

> We rose early and took the chief to the public store, and furnished him with some clothes, etc. We took an early breakfast with Colonel Hunt and set out. We descended to the Mississippi and down that river to St. Louis, at which place we arrived about 12 o'clock. We suffered the party to fire off their pieces as a salute to the town. We were met by all the village and received a hearty welcome from its inhabitants. Here I found my old acquaintance Major W. Christy who had settled in this town in a public line as a tavern keeper. He furnished us with storerooms for our baggage. We accepted of the invitation of Mr. Peter Chouteau and took a room in his house. We paid a friendly visit to Mr. August Chouteau and some of our old friends this evening.
>
> *Clark, September 23, 1806*

Clark took the rest of the group from Traveler's Rest over Lemhi Pass to Three Forks. From there, Ordway took one group with the canoes back down the Missouri, and Clark took the remaining 12 people down the Yellowstone River. Clark had planned to ride horses to the mouth of the Yellowstone, but Gibson was injured when a horse threw him. Because Gibson couldn't ride, they made canoes and sent Pryor with three men to take the horses while the rest of the group descended the Yellowstone in canoes.

The Crow Indians stole the horses from Pryor on their second night out. Pryor's group then made two buffalo skin boats and floated down the Yellowstone River behind Clark. They caught up with Clark on the Missouri River on August 8. Lewis caught up with Clark four days later. Cruzatte accidentally shot Lewis in the butt, mistaking him for an elk, the day before they reached Clark. Lewis recovered, but he couldn't walk for several days.

As the expedition descended the Missouri, they began to meet some traders and received their first news in two years. They were told that most of the country had given them up for lost, but not the President. On September 23, 1806, Lewis and Clark reached St. Louis. People lined the banks, cheering.

> I slept but little last night; however, we rose early and commenced writing our letters. Captain Lewis wrote one to the President and I wrote Governor Harrison and my friends in Kentucky. We dined with Mr. Chouteau today, and after dinner went to a store and purchased some clothes which we gave to a tailor and directed to be made. Captain Lewis in opening his trunk found all his papers wet, and some seeds spoiled.
>
> *Clark, September 24, 1806*

> We paid some visits of form to the gentlemen of St. Louis. In the evening was a dinner and ball.
>
> *Clark, September 25, 1806*

A fine morning. We
commenced writing, etc.
Clark, September 26, 1806

About the Plane

The Aircam has an open cockpit, two seats, and two "pusher" engines. It cruises at 60 to 80 mph, with a minimum speed of about 41 mph. It can safely land in less than 300 feet, and on takeoff leaves the ground in less than 100 feet. The engines are 100 horsepower each, and the plane flies well on only one engine. With the security of two engines, slow speed, and a wide-open cockpit, the Aircam was the ideal plane for *Lewis and Clark by Air*.

In August of 2000, our Aircam was delivered in a box marked not "Fragile," but "Aircraft, Expensive." The three of us who built it had no experience in airplane maintenance, let alone construction. We forged ahead anyway.

In the building process, we outfitted the plane with complete IFR instrumentation for flying in clouds and low visibility. After six months of hard work, the plane not only flew, but also landed safely. We thought the latter very important.

The Aircam is really fun to fly. The seats in the Aircam leave both people flying out in the open, ahead of the engines and the rest of the plane. It is a thrilling experience, and offers outstanding visibility. The

Aircam has the power to climb at very steep angles, and can ascend to more than 17,500 feet. It can descend at

more than 3,000 feet per minute, and has no trouble accessing short and unimproved airstrips.

Soon after we departed the Claremore, Oklahoma Airport, where the plane is based, for St. Louis, we checked the stall speed. The Aircam is a light plane, and the stall speed is influenced significantly by the amount of weight in the plane. We stalled at 35 mph.

On our way to St. Louis, we decided to climb over some rain clouds at about 7,000 feet. As we progressed to the northeast, the cloud tops got higher. When we got to 14,000 feet we realized we weren't going to climb over the clouds. We got IFR clearance from the air traffic controller, descended through the clouds, and flew through the rain for a while. In rain, the person in front stays relatively dry behind the windshield, but a passenger in back gets a bit wet. After the first day, we were on the Lewis and Clark Trail and avoided rainy weather. Photography, rain, and an open-cockpit airplane are not a good mix.

At 14,000 feet, the temperature was in the 30's. In a windy, open cockpit, that gets really cold. Sitting in the wind with very little body movement makes even 60 degrees seem cold after an hour or so. We used plenty of warm clothes on our trip. More than once, after descending from higher altitudes, we raised some eyebrows when we climbed out of the plane dressed in our winter suits, hats, and gloves into 90 degree heat or more on the ground.

The range of the Aircam between fuel stops is around 200 or 250 miles, depending on airspeed and altitude. On our trip down the Lewis and Clark Trail we had very little trouble finding airports for fuel. In a sparsely populated area of Montana, we carried two gasoline cans with us so we could stop and refuel between the airports that sold fuel. In Orofino, Idaho, we started walking into town for gasoline and caught a ride with one of the friendly people there. On the rest of the trip to the Pacific, we had no trouble getting from airport to airport with plenty vof fuel reserves.

Before we left home we fabricated a rear windshield that was a little wider than the original, in order to keep more of the wind off the rear passenger. Hours of vibration caused some cracks to develop, which we fixed with glue, silicon rubber, and finally part of an aluminum carpenter's square. The carpenter's square is still on the plane today, reinforcing a new rear windshield.

The entire trip, Oklahoma-St. Louis-Oregon-Oklahoma, took about 70 hours in the air. The only mechanical problems we had were fouled spark plugs and a cracked rear windshield.

The Rotax engines on the Aircam are 4-stroke engines designed to run on unleaded premium gasoline. Most airports only sell avgas, which contains quite a bit of lead additive. The Rotax engines run fine with avgas (aviation gasoline), but this causes the spark plugs to foul sooner than normal.

Aircam Specifications	
Horsepower	2 * 100
Gross Weight	1,680 lbs.
Empty Weight	1,090 lbs.
Stall Speed (max weight)	41 mph
Minimum Single Engine Speed	42 mph
Maximum Speed	110 mph
Cruise Speed	50 to 100 mph
Fuel Capacity	28 gallons
Range	340 miles

During our return to Oklahoma we stopped in Leadville, Colorado, the highest airport in the United States. In the background is Mount Elbert, the highest peak in Colorado.

Glossary

avgas — Aviation gasoline, 100 octane low lead.

blaireau — French word for badger.

bluff — A high, steep bank or cliff.

bow — The front of a boat.

brant — Any of a number of types of small geese.

buffalo — Common name for American bison, and also a type of fish.

cable — A rope.

cache — A place in which to store food or supplies.

camera obscura — A pinhole camera that projects an image onto a surface opposite the pinhole, often used for sketching.

carrot of tobacco — A twist or roll of tobacco leaves resembling a carrot.

cascade — A small, steep waterfall, especially one of a series.

cupola — A dome structure.

dram — A small drink of alcoholic liquor.

flag — A plant with long, thin leaves, such as a reed, rush, or iris.

hackmatack — A juniper or tamarack tree.

ibex — One of several varieties of wild goats with large, curved horns.

larboard — The left side of a boat.

league — An imprecise measurement of distance, usually about 3 miles.

parallelepiped — A 3-dimensional box-like shape in which each side is a parallelogram.

parallelogram — A four-sided polygon with each opposite pair of sides parallel.

parroquet — Parakeet.

pipe tomahawk — A tomahawk with a pipe built into the handle, used for ceremonial smoking.

pirogue — Lewis and Clark used this term for a boat larger than their canoes.

prairie wolf — Lewis and Clark's name for coyote.

quamash — Camas, a member of the lily family with edible roots, or the bread made from those roots.

S 25° W — This notation means 25 degrees west of straight south, or south-south-west.

snag — An underwater tree or log that presents a danger to navigation.

spontoon — A military spear sometimes carried by Lewis and Clark.

starboard — The right side of a boat.

stern — The rear of a boat.

wampum — Small beads used by the Indians for money and ornament. This term sometimes applies to other small items of merchandise traded or given to the Indians.

weir — A brush fence across a stream for catching fish.

withe — A slender, flexible branch use as a rope.

wye — A Y-shaped railroad switch.

Index